More Praise for

"If ever there was a time when the Methodist church needed a guidebook to usher in calm, it is now. In five practical steps, *Calm: How to End Destructive Conflict in Your Church* helps congregations navigate change and develop healthier communities. Thoroughly researched and thoughtfully written, this consensus-based, congregation-led curriculum offers the healing and hope that so many of our churches need."

—Glenys Nellist, lifelong Methodist and author of five popular series for children: Love Letters from God, Little Mole, 'Twas, Good News, and Snuggle Time

"The authors understand conflict in the church, both its creative possibilities and its potential harm. While deeply rooted in theory, this book is eminently practical, providing a detailed five-module curriculum for working with conflict through critical conversations, all in the service of building healthier communities. While particularly useful in the midst of conflict, I encourage pastors and church leaders to engage this material before conflict becomes intense. Your everyday leadership will benefit from the insights and tools offered by these three wise guides."

—David A. Bard, bishop, Michigan Conference of The United Methodist Church

"As an organizational researcher and consultant, I was delighted to see how well-grounded in research *Calm: How to End Destructive Conflict in Your Church* is. As a lifelong United Methodist, I wish that this valuable resource had been available in many of the congregations I've been part of. Mary Gladstone-Highland, Katy Stokes, and Christina Wichert have provided a step-by-step guide that churches facing any major decisions will find practical and helpful."

—Marcus Dickson, Professor of Industrial/Organizational Psychology, Wayne State University, Detroit, MI

"This is a treasure trove for anyone preparing to lead a congregation in a process of conflict resolution. It gives practical, wholistic, and multi-disciplinary ideas that assist in identifying the root causes of conflict in a church. It includes tips on how to lead a virtual conversation as well, which is a timely new reality. The detail and scholarship in this book will enable any leader (lay or clergy) to have critical conversations that can achieve a healthy consensus."

—Peggy A. Johnson, retired bishop, Northeastern Jurisdiction, The United Methodist Church

"Calm: How to End Destructive Conflict in Your Church offers a remarkable journey into spiritual discovery and reflection, creating an intimate space where faith and personal introspection intersect. As a reader, I found the engaging, carefully crafted prayer stations stirring a deeper understanding of my spiritual identity and role in addressing conflict proactively in my ministry. Through its innovative approach to prayer and reflection, the book serves as an exceptional guide, cultivating an environment of empathy, gratitude, and action."

—Beverly A. Browning (Dr. Bev), Grant Writing Training Foundation, Integro Bank Governing Board Member and Integro Bank Foundation Executive Director

"Calm: How to End Destructive Conflict in Your Church delivers a clearly defined process and strategies to work through heated conflicts in your church. Critical components include the choice of leaders to guide this process, hospitable spaces to meet, participants who do not succumb to 'groupthink,' and a willingness to commit time, energy, and creativity to navigate intractable situations. What makes this approach work is the belief that every participant has a voice, and every voice is equal. *Calm* can help you move forward beyond any conflict."

—Charlene P. Kammerer, retired bishop, Southeastern Jurisdiction, The United Methodist Church

Mary Gladstone-Highland
Katy Stokes
Christina Wichert

Calm

How to End Destructive Conflict in Your Church

Abingdon Press™

Nashville

CALM:
HOW TO END DESTRUCTIVE CONFLICT IN YOUR CHURCH

Copyright © 2023 by Abingdon Press

ISBN: 9781791030247

Library of Congress Control Number has been requested.

Scripture quotations marked (NRSVue) are taken from the New Revised Standard Version Updated Edition. Copyright © 2021 National Council of Churches of Christ in the United States of America. Used by permission. All rights reserved worldwide.

Scripture quotations marked (NIV) are taken from the Holy Bible, New International Version®, NIV®. Copyright © 1973, 1978, 1984, 2011 by Biblica, Inc.™ Used by permission of Zondervan. All rights reserved worldwide. www.zondervan.com The "NIV" and "New International Version" are trademarks registered in the United States Patent and Trademark Office by Biblica, Inc.™

Scripture quotations marked (NASB) are taken from the New American Standard Bible® (NASB), Copyright © 1960, 1962, 1963, 1968, 1971, 1972, 1973, 1975, 1977, 1995 by The Lockman Foundation. Used by permission. www.Lockman.org.

Scripture quotations marked (KJV) are taken from The Authorized (King James) Version. Rights in the Authorized Version in the United Kingdom are vested in the Crown. Reproduced by permission of the Crown's patentee, Cambridge University Press.

Scripture quotations marked (ESV) are from the ESV Bible (The Holy Bible, English Standard Version®), copyright © 2001 by Crossway, a publishing ministry of Good News Publishers. Used by permission. All rights reserved.

MANUFACTURED IN THE UNITED STATES OF AMERICA

Contents

Introduction

Conflicts can be incredibly hard to navigate. When not handled well, they can create division and harm faith communities, but that doesn't need to be the case. You probably picked up this book because you are in the middle of a conflict at your church, or because you know someone similarly struggling. You likely feel tired and lost, searching for a guidebook to resolve the tension.

In these chapters, you will learn how to help your church address conflict through critical conversations that lead to thriving faith communities. This text includes five modules you can use to create healthier conflict resolution. *Calm* offers a step-by-step curriculum so that you have all the tools and resources necessary within these pages to address your conflict proactively and create a future path forward.

Meet the Authors

You might want to know a little about who "we"—the authors—are before we begin. This book is co-authored by three women, all lifelong United Methodists, who each bring a unique angle to conflict work and ministry.

Mary Gladstone-Highland has spent twelve years serving as a domestic missionary for the General Board of Global Ministries. She has been a panel expert for regional and jurisdictional conferences, has worked on issues that affect the denomination internationally, and is committed to helping churches to be healthy and thriving witnesses of Christ's love. A graduate of the Maxwell

School of Citizenship and Public Affairs at Syracuse University, she holds a master of public administration and a certificate in advanced study in conflict and collaboration and is also a mediator with the state of Michigan.

Christina Wichert has spent over a decade navigating the unique team dynamics present in multicultural environments in the US and abroad. Her specialty in church conflict resolution is grounded in a dual MA/MTS degree from Wesley Seminary and American University—School of International Service in Washington DC, with a concentration in international peace and conflict resolution. Additionally, she holds a graduate certificate in sustainable development from the American University in Cairo, Egypt. A former GBGM domestic missionary, Christina is dedicated to supporting God's just and wonderful community, inside and outside the walls of the church.

Katy Stokes is a community and clinical social worker with a master's degree from Wayne State University in macro social work, with a concentration in leadership development. She worked for twelve years with The United Methodist Church in the Michigan area at the local and conference levels in the area of worship arts, family programming, and program development. Katy works as a child and family therapist and supervises a team of behavioral health consultants. She is committed to helping people make changes in their lives and their communities through open communication and self-awareness.

Together, our backgrounds complement one another's, to view conflict and conflict resolution from different angles, and present a curriculum that looks to the holistic needs of the church body as well the individuals who make up that body. We support churches with practical ways of moving forward out of conflict, while also acknowledging and honoring the pain, trauma, and need for healing caused by conflict, and sometimes the path forward that is chosen.

How Does Conflict Hurt Churches?

There are several unhealthy ways that conflict may show up in your local church. First, when you don't have all of the skills and tools necessary to address disagreements in a healthy way, then it is easy to create teams and "other" people. Think of times you've heard phrases like, "They don't understand," or "We do it right, but they refuse to follow the rules." These divisions make it hard to find a solution everyone can support—meaning, there will always be winners and losers.

Another way unhealthy conflict resolution shows up in faith communities is that people ignore the issue to keep the peace. But avoidance doesn't make the conflict go away. It only covers it up and brushes it under the rug. Often these tensions come back with renewed passion because they were never addressed in the first place. When you hear people say, "We shouldn't argue. This is church. We should all get along," that is an example of conflict avoidance. While it seems like the easy option, it rarely resolves tensions and can eventually make matters worse.

This curriculum asks congregations to lean into the hard work of creating an intentional community, or as Dr. Martin Luther King Jr. often described, a "beloved community."[1] Though we recognize that conflict is "an inevitable part of human experience," as Dr. King taught, reconciliation remains possible through a determined commitment to community building.[2]

The material we've created asks participants to break down divisions, learn from one another, and commit to solving the issue together. We make a case for the benefits of addressing conflict head-on, give you examples of how to make collective decisions without voting, and offer a detailed guide for facilitating the curriculum—all that you need to offer the material in your church, whether in person or virtually.

Understanding the Curriculum

Calm deploys five modules to shepherd your church members through a process of deeper understanding and collaboration. Working through the modules can help your church gain the skills and tools necessary to engage in critical conversations that lead to healthy communities and remain

---

1. "Six Steps of Nonviolent Social Change," The King Center; https://thekingcenter.org/about-tkc/the-king-philosophy/.

2. "Six Steps of Nonviolent Change."

God-focused in times of conflict and tension. The five modules you will encounter are:

Module One: Acknowledging the Struggle

Module Two: Understanding the Paths Forward

Module Three: Making Informed and Collective Decisions

Module Four: Honoring the Process

Module Five: Mapping the Path Forward

Before you begin, you can use the planning resources in the back of the book to help you organize logistics.

Module Outline

The process begins in Module One by identifying the issue and building an intentional community and shared group culture. This first module also asks participants to establish boundaries for their time together and define a shared vision statement.

In the second module, Understanding the Paths Forward, the participants will name the different ways church members experience the issue's impact individually and collectively and will think creatively to generate possible solutions. They will then identify significant themes and discuss where the energy in your congregation is leaning.

The third module is where the material shifts from theoretical to practical. The curriculum frees up issues that are stuck in indecision. It uses a method of collective decision-making intentionally different from voting, which inherently creates winners and losers. Instead, this process asks the participants to choose a solution that all participants can support.

After a decision is made, it is time for worship. The fourth module celebrates the process and participants. It names God's movement in the commitment to the hard work of conflict resolution and holds space for those who might not be able to sign on to the chosen path forward. The module is a worshipful, prayerful, reflective time that honors not only the hard work being done but also the perspectives of all individuals who participated.

The final module calls on the participants to lay the groundwork necessary to achieve the intended solution. It offers confidence to the participants by outlining the hard work of the process so that no one's time is wasted. The material leaves churches with actionable steps and a clear map for the journey forward.

Practical Application

At this point, you may be asking, "How can I offer the material to my church?" Great question! We began working on this material in 2018. Therefore, we initially envisioned events in fellowship halls, tables lined with desserts and a hot coffee pot bubbling away . . . and then the pandemic hit.

To pivot, we shifted our focus for this curriculum and adapted it to a virtual setting. The result was that all modules now have an in-person and virtual adaptation for you to offer in the format that suits your participants best. You can look out for instructions marked Virtual Adaptation if your group is utilizing a virtual meeting space such as Zoom.

Additionally, the material is offered in modules to be flexible to your ministry setting. You can offer the modules on Monday nights for five weeks, on three Saturdays, or as a retreat. In each module, we offer a suggested length and pattern to follow but also allow you to adapt the material to meet your needs.

When writing this curriculum and text, we asked ourselves two questions: "Could this activity be used to help a congregation that is struggling over whether or not to launch a contemporary worship service?" and "Could this activity also be used to help a congregation determining their steps forward during the potential denominational schism?"

In using those two lenses, we made sure to develop modules that could be used in any church argument, whether big or small. Additionally, the material provides your church members with the skills to address future conflicts with greater confidence and collaboration.

If your church is embroiled in conflict, then you know that it has the potential to damage your ministries. Think of the times you witnessed disagreements regarding who should manage aspects of worship. There are often tensions over space, altar designs, and calendaring. These may seem like smaller issues, but they make it tense to lead worship. Conversely, your congregants might be arguing over deep theological differences. Larger arguments also have the capability to stale ministry work. Simply put, when your church members are stuck, focusing on a conflict, their attention is captured, making it harder to focus on the church's mission.

What This Book Isn't

This book helps you identify the root causes of conflict, engage your church in deeper learning, and craft a solution together. However, it is important to note that there are a few things that this text won't offer.

First and foremost, this material does not stop all conflict from happening in your church. There is no magic wand for you to wave and magically "poof" conflict away. Arguments and tensions will arise in your congregation because it comprises people. Those children of God make right and wrong decisions. They have passions, and they have faults. And that is a good thing! It means that God truly loves us as we are, and we can bring our true selves to church. Additionally, your church is part of a district, conference, or denomination that also makes right and wrong decisions. These institutions have assets and faults too, and because of that, conflicts will arise.

This book is also not intended to choose a side in your conflict. You will not find the right or wrong answers to the tension in your ministry setting within these pages. We have developed this curriculum to be used again and again in all sorts of applications—in small conflicts and large conflicts. Instead, this is a process or a framework for addressing those conflicts and creating healthy communities by handling those conflicts together with your congregation.

Finally, this book won't prescribe your solution, unfortunately—no matter how much you may want it to. You will not find a step-by-step list of what you, as the reader, need to do for your specific conflict to create your best path forward. This material needs the input of those church members on both sides of your issue to create your path forward together. For that reason, there is no one-size-fits-all option. Instead, it gives you the tools for solving your tension in community with your fellow church members.

Who Can Use This Book

Because this text deals with church conflicts, you might wonder if the curriculum is only for clergy or church staff. This book is intended for anyone who has a heart and a passion for proactively resolving their church's conflicts. Therefore, you might have picked up this book because you're a clergyperson. You know of a conflict that's happening within your church and want the tools to help your church address it. Or maybe you know of a fellow clergy colleague who is struggling to address an issue in their local church.

You might be on your church's staff and looking for tools to help the church members in your congregation address conflict. Or maybe you are a church leader. You're in charge of a committee or a team, and you think this might be useful to help you navigate change. Additionally, you might be a district superintendent or on your annual conference's staff and looking for ways to support churches in your area in handling conflicts that arise. If that is the case, then this material is helpful as a train-the-trainer tool to offer support to struggling congregations.

You can also use this book as a small-group study, even if you aren't actively experiencing conflict in your ministry setting. For example, a youth group, women's circle, or Sunday School class could decide to dive into this text. Each chapter offers reflection questions to give your church the skills that they might need in the future when conflicts arise. If you are the director of a camping and retreat center and you are putting on events, you may consider using this material as an event or retreat for United Methodists in your area to learn about conflict resolution skills. In essence, there are tons of ways and applications for this material because we intended it to be flexible to your unique ministry setting.

When conflict arises in church congregations, the path forward is often uncertain. This can lead to feelings of anxiety and stress, invoking a "fight or flight" response. Uncertainty can stoke the flames of conflict to even greater levels (fight) or cripple the church body into a state of stasis, of doing nothing or avoidance (flight). *Calm* frames the conflict resolution process as finding a path forward when difficult decisions—big or small—need to be made. The book's five modules illuminate that path forward. Working through the modules, you will gain the skills and tools necessary to engage groups in critical conversations that lead to healthy communities that remain God-focused in times of conflict and tension.

Collective Decision-Making

Later in this book you will find the five modules that walk you through the process of shepherding a group or congregation with *Calm*. You'll notice upon reaching the modules that collective decision-making happens in Module Three—at the very middle point of the process. Making the decision exactly halfway through the process is intentional. This provides the group ample time and opportunity to first build a safe space together and establish a group culture where individuals can trust one another and feel comfortable expressing their thoughts and opinions. It also provides space after the decision has been made for the group to reflect on that decision in a worship setting, offering up any anxieties or insecurities still being felt around the decision, as well as acknowledging and repenting for any real pain the decision will cause members of the community. The final module then guides the group in creating a roadmap of steps necessary to build around the decision made, to begin to move forward.

You'll notice as well that Module Three points groups toward using a different model of collective decision-making than the ones participants may expect to use or be used to using. In other words, Module Three explains how to make a decision without using the traditional voting method. This move away from voting is also intentional.

Before we explain why we use an alternative method to voting, we must acknowledge that in some scenarios, for some decisions, groups will find themselves having to vote. These scenarios are ones in which bylaws, articles of incorporation, or other governing documents stipulate that certain decision must be made by vote. Let's face it, voting is often enthroned as "the" method of collective decision-making used by groups seeking to be fair or democratic, and is therefore incorporated into organizational standards or rules of order. So, if your bylaws say you have to hold a vote, then vote! You can still follow the directives in Module Three but replace the collective decision-making process outline there with the required vote, following the rules of your congregation or organization. And we will cover this more in Module Three.

But outside of those scenarios where voting is specifically required by bylaws, we are convinced there is a better way to move forward when it comes to collective decision-making. Let us explain.

Voting: The Pros and Cons

There's no denying it—voting is firmly entrenched in American culture. From preschool age onward, group or collective decisions are made by voting. Think back to childhood and consider how many times a quick raised-hand-count was the deciding factor in what book to read for story time, what game to play, what movie to watch . . . the list goes on and on. And while teachers, parents, or other adults introduce children to the concept of voting, think how quickly and easily the voting process is taken up by young children. Almost as soon as kids learn to count, and learn to compare "greater than" and "less than," they learn how to vote!

And doesn't that describe the beauty of voting? It's fast, it's easy, it's efficient, and it's simple. Encounter a decision to be made, propose the options, count, and decide! And for the most part, once a vote is counted, the outcome of that vote is generally considered fair. At least (or should we say *especially?*) by the winning majority, that outcome is considered fair, but more on that later.

It's really no exaggeration to say that entire countries have been established around the cornerstone of voting. And institutions in and of those countries—including churches—have followed suit. As mentioned in the introduction to this chapter, for many organizations, clubs, churches, and so on, bylaws and articles of incorporation typically lay out exactly how voting should take place. And typically, as we all know, voting rules stipulate a winner-take-all outcome.

And so the issue begins to emerge—especially as we consider collective decision-making in a church context. It's not to say that voting is inherently bad or problematic; as we pointed out earlier, there are clear benefits to decision-making by voting. But churches can and should be a place to reflect on why we adopt the practices and habits that we do: "And do not be conformed to this world, but be transformed by the renewing of your mind, so that you may prove what the will of God is, that which is good and acceptable and perfect" (Romans 12:2 NASB). And reflecting on why we typically make collective, group decisions by voting, we might ask: The benefits to voting might indeed make things simpler, faster, and more efficient, but at what cost?

Consider this scenario: Your church is trying to decide whether or not to change the time of a Sunday worship service. Thirty people are present for the vote. Sixteen individuals vote in favor of changing the time, and fourteen vote against ending. In a simple majority-rule situation, the change is adopted, even though that majority only represents the opinion of 53 percent of those who voted. (And this is somewhat generous; in some instances, majority-rule votes can carry with only a 51 percent or even 50.99 percent majority.)

So, a decision is carried that, true, over half of those present to vote supported. But were those in favor *strongly* in favor? Or did folks without any strong feelings on the issue vote because of how the issue was presented in the meeting? Maybe those who opposed, opposed strongly, but just didn't have the numbers on their side on that particular evening. Who was present to vote? Were the people who could be affected most by the change invited or able to attend the vote? The people who have the farthest to drive might be most challenged by the time change, or maybe elderly congregants or families with young children, and these same people could very well also have the hardest time attending a meeting or being on a committee where the vote on the issue takes place. In other words, was deciding by voting truly "fair"?

Majority-rule situations can easily silence a significant number of voices and trample over opinions. It's no wonder, then, that decisions by majority-rule voting can leave a bad taste in folks' mouths, at best, and can cause real trauma to those who feel unheard and unvalued by the church body, at worst.

Has anyone really "won" in such a scenario? For these reasons, we strongly encourage churches not to give up voting completely, but to consider, explore, and adopt other methods of collective decision-making whenever possible.

Consensus: The Pros and Cons

An alternative way to make a decision collectively is to reach consensus. In order to reach a true consensus, each individual involved in the process voices a position. Ultimately, everyone involved agrees to support the final decision made, though it may not be everyone's favorite choice. Reaching consensus takes a large amount of dedicated buy-in up front, as those involved must commit to making a decision that's best for the group as a whole, instead of competing for their own personal preferences.

There are many different ways and means of reaching consensus for both large and small group settings. If you're interested in exploring the subject more, the Session Lab (https://wp.sessionlab.com/) is a great online resource, with a library of facilitation methods and practices for consensus-building and collective decision-making.

Let's be clear: compared to voting, reaching consensus takes much more effort and time. Consensus-building generally also requires the role of a third-party facilitator to keep the process on track. Transparently speaking, some may even describe the process as tedious, and sometimes reaching consensus can be uncomfortable and contentious. But the group's commitment to hearing all voices and buying-in to the process from start to finish highly increase the likelihood of reaching a successful outcome.

The Dangers of Groupthink

A word of caution: Sometimes what is thought of as "consensus" may actually be something else quite different: a group dynamic known as "groupthink." This dynamic was first described by psychologist Irving Janis in 1971, though it carries echoes of the satirical "doublethink" of George Orwell's famous novel, *1984*. Groupthink occurs when "loyalty [to the group] requires each member to avoid raising controversial issues,"[1] which results in a decision made "without critical thinking or an evaluation of the possible consequences or alternatives."[2] In other words, groupthink occurs because group members want to seem agreeable, are afraid to voice their opinion, and avoid ruffling feathers.

The desire to maintain group cohesion, which can provide a sense of safety and belonging, is a strong one and isn't necessarily a problem in itself. But groupthink often happens due to strong outside pressure, coming either from a strong and persuasive leader or from the group itself. Groupthink can cause individuals to put aside their personal beliefs and adopt the majority option, which does not represent true consensus.

Going back to the example used earlier, imagine a church who is again trying to reach a decision around changing the Sunday worship service time. Church leaders are trying to reach a consensual decision and have invited the congregation to discuss the different options. The discussion seems to be going smoothly at first, with some speaking for and against the change openly and respectfully of one another. And then John Doe speaks up. His family has been a part of the church since its doors first opened (as he often likes to remind people) and has been generous with their wealth when it comes to supporting church ministries. He is against the change. He speaks firmly, though not derisively. But after he speaks, the once-robust debate quickly simmers. Little more than some meekly affirmative head-nods—though maybe with pursed lips and downward glances—come from those who, prior to Doe's arrival, had been in favor of the change. That's groupthink.

Facilitators leading groups in consensus-building should look out for signs that groupthink may be at play, such as one individual or cohort seeming to stifle discussion or wield influence in such a way that others seem hesitant to contradict them. If these things begin to happen, there are ways to counteract the power dynamics at play. Break into smaller groups to dis-

---

1. I. L. Janis, *Groupthink*, 2nd ed. (Boston: Houghton Mifflin, 1982), cited by J. D. Rose, "Diverse Perspectives on the Groupthink Theory–A Literary Review," *Emerging Leadership Journeys* 4, no. 1: 37–57.

2. "Groupthink," The Decision Lab; https://thedecisionlab.com/reference-guide /management/groupthink.

cuss issues separately. Continue to give group members regular opportunities to share their ideas and thoughts. Provide opportunities to share ideas or thoughts anonymously.

Reaching Consensus with *Calm*

The *Calm* curriculum you hold is a guide to collective decision-making through consensus. Working through the modules together, your church members who participate will make a commitment to the process, establish a culture of trust and respect, voice their positions, and hear and be heard by others, specifically throughout the first two modules. When you reach Module Three, it will be time to make your collective decision. We explain how to do so using our favorite collective decision-making tool.

The tool and process we describe in Module Three are based on the Feedback Frame system, developed and patented by Jason Diceman of Toronto, Canada, in 2014. For the simplest application of the system, you can visit the website feedbackframes.com to purchase a Feedback Frames kit. We love this method because it recognizes "nuanced gradients of agreement towards consensus," while providing instant and powerful visual results. Participants use physical tokens to indicate on a 1 to 5 scale how strongly they favor or disfavor each presented option for going forward. The tokens are placed in a covered receptacle representing their preference at each voting station, one per option presented. When the ranking process has ended, the covers are removed and the results are revealed. Though the tokens are certainly counted and scored, the displayed array of physical tokens provides a clear, visual indication of where the group has landed, even before counts and calculations are made.

Why One Size Might Not Fit All

Module Three is similar to the rest of our curriculum in that we outline the objective (collective decision-making) and then describe a process we've found successful for meeting that objective. We also describe how and why the process we outline successfully meets the objective. We understand there may be circumstances in which a different or modified process of collective decision-making is right for your church's context. As we said at the start of the chapter, it may be that the decision your church is making requires a vote. That's okay. Even if you have to hold a vote, by working through Modules One and Two, you're putting in the legwork necessary for reaching a consensus. And even if you have to use a different method of decision-making, don't stop working through the last two modules. What's important isn't that you make a collective decision in a certain way. However, it is important that you make a decision and move forward; otherwise, you'll end up right back where you started, languishing in the mires and tension of unresolved conflict.

Reflection Questions

If your aim is to address an active conflict within your church, consider these questions:

1. Does my church require a vote over the issue in conflict?

2. If it does require a vote, how can we make sure more diverse voices are heard in the voting process?

3. If it does not require a vote, what support do I need to implement the collective decision-making process outlined in this chapter?

4. What is my first step?

If your aim is to proactively outfit your church with healthy conflict-resolution skills, consider these questions:

1. How does our congregation typically make collective decisions?

2. Try to think of the last time a collective decision was made. Would you describe the process as particularly fair? Why or why not?

3. How easy or challenging would it be to adopt a different method of decision-making, like the one described in this chapter? What would be some of the challenges?

4. What stands out to you in this chapter? What do you notice?

Notes

Why Cultural Context Matters

We can't really write a book about resolving conflict without touching on a key aspect of conflict resolution—that is, cultural context. Churches can hardly be successful in navigating a path forward through conflict without taking cultural context into account. This is true even when church members share a similar cultural background, but it is especially true when church members come from different cultural backgrounds. Generally speaking, people from different cultures experience or interpret conflict differently and have different ideas and practices about how to resolve conflict.

The Culture Iceberg

But what exactly do we mean when we talk about cultural context? There's a famous visual representation used to describe culture; perhaps you've seen it? The image illustrates a concept first developed by Edward T. Hall in 1976—the concept of culture as an iceberg. Just as only an iceberg's small tip can be seen above the surface of the water while the majority of the iceberg's mass remains unseen, only a small component of culture is easily visible or recognizable (surface culture), while most of what makes up culture (internal or deep culture) remains hidden below the surface. Together, these surface and internal components of culture help shape our behaviors, values, and beliefs.

When we are asked to reflect on culture, for most of us, it's those surface elements of culture we think about first: the traditions, customs, holidays, food, dress, music, and so on. The cultural elements hidden below the surface don't typically initially come to mind. But like the bulk of the iceberg, it's the hidden mass under the surface that carries the most "weight" and can have the biggest impact on group dynamics. So, we must dive deeper to carefully consider what can easily be forgotten or overlooked.

These are just some of the elements of deep culture that can shape the ways groups navigate conflict: verbal and nonverbal communication styles, identity formation, concepts of self as an individual and as a member of a collective, norms around sharing or displaying emotions, power dynamics and attitudes towards authority, and practices regarding conflict and even conflict resolution itself. There's lots of information and research on this subject available for anyone interested in learning more. One interesting place to start is Geert Hofstede's early work on the subject, *Cultures and Organizations: Software of the Mind.*

When facilitator and participants understand the factors that may be shaping the dynamics of their group, if they take the time to build trust and establish good communication practices and treat one another with respect, a path forward through conflict can emerge.

Who Does "Culture" Belong To?

Another thing to keep in mind is that culture is something that belongs to a group of people, not to an individual. As much as we might want to try sometimes, we can't really talk about culture in terms of a single individual— even ourselves! True, we may talk about the concept of "my own culture." But even in this situation, when talking about or describing "your" culture, you're really speaking of something greater than you. You're inherently relating to a wider group of people and to the beliefs, understandings, and traditions you share with that group. If this wasn't the case, then you'd simply be describing your own quirks and characteristics, not your culture.

All of this is to say that when we describe culture and how it relates to group dynamics, we are talking broadly about general patterns, using a macro lens. We are not talking specifically about any individual, or prescribing how an individual thinks or behaves. In other words, we don't assume, "Well, [insert name here] is a part of *x culture*, so this means they will think or do *y*," which can lead to an even worse line of thinking: "Since we know what they are going to say or do, we don't really need to invite them." Assumptions about individuals only lead to further conflict. Besides, a key tenet of building a consensus is that each person gets to speak for themselves.

Culture and the Curriculum

So, what does this mean for our curriculum? Well first, there are a few things it doesn't mean!

Cultural diversity is not the root of conflict. It's also not an excuse to avoid seeking resolution. Churches stagnate by adopting "us versus them" mentality and saying things like, "It's no use to talk to *them*, they are just so different, they'll never understand *us*." On the contrary, cultural differences provide a wider perspective to examine and try to understand the root causes of conflict, and seek a resolution. Diverse groups tend to generate diverse ideas, which increases the chances that a successful path forward will emerge. Diverse groups also tend to avoid the problem of groupthink. Sure, the journey towards consensus may take a little longer or a little extra care, and it might look a little messier from the outside. But the outcome is worth it! Therefore, a diversity of backgrounds and contexts should be welcomed and celebrated. If your church members come from many different backgrounds, this is a wonderful blessing!

With all that in mind, here are some tips for facilitators and participants navigating the curriculum with an eye to cultural context.

Acknowledge Your Own Biases

It's important to acknowledge we each have a set of our own cultural biases, and sometimes we might get things wrong. As hard as we may try not to, it's easy to slip up and operate as if our own perspective is the standard perspective, or our own context is the standard context. This is something we had to remember even when writing this book. With an early draft of the modules, we received some feedback that some of the ice-breaker activities might not work in certain cultural contexts where some people might not feel comfortable speaking about what's on their hearts or minds outside of family. We welcomed that feedback, and the reminder that a shift of perspective was needed. And more importantly, we made a correction. We added another option. So yes, you might get things wrong during the process sometimes too. That's okay, as long as you stay open to receiving feedback with grace and correcting course when necessary. Reaching group consensus doesn't demand perfection; it's a process that calls for honest and open communication and respect.

Create a Group Culture

Another important element of successfully navigating cultural context and reaching consensus is creating a microculture amongst your working group. This microculture is created when your group has a shared understanding of purpose, boundaries, values, and goals, when group members have developed trust in one another and synergy. When this group microculture is created, it doesn't supplant or replace other understandings of culture. But it does give the group a common touchstone to share as your congregation together navigates new ways of communicating ideas, shaping identity, sharing emotions, and understanding power dynamics (those aspects of deep culture we talked about earlier) in the curriculum process.

In fact, the curriculum's Module One is designed for this very purpose of building an intentional community and shared group culture together. We designed and selected activities to slowly and intentionally bring the group together as a cohesive unit, with the aim of building the trust necessary for folks to feel safe having tough conversations later on and to share what's truly on their hearts and minds. We can't jump right into the deepest waters of the conflict, but we can't let everyone just puddle about in the shallows, never leaving their comfort zone, either.

Another reason for creating a shared group culture is that the group culture should be wholly different; it should not align with any other culture. Facilitators from a dominant or majority culture need to take extra care to heed this point. Ideally, everyone in the group should feel a little discomfort at times—a sign that the process is moving them beyond their comfort zone. But no participants should feel discomfort at all times—a sign that the group culture created is not different enough from a culture foreign to those feeling constant discomfort.

Your Voice Matters

Churches who most successfully apply this curriculum will be the ones who value the voice and perspective of each and every person who chooses to participate. They will also be the churches who do the outreach so that a diverse group of people actually make that choice to participate.

We discussed earlier in this chapter, how an "us versus them" mentality can lead to churches stagnating in conflict. We talked about the group who says "They don't think like us, so they shouldn't be invited to the process," and how that cripples the conflict-resolution process. But even when "they" are invited—whoever they may be—they aren't likely to show up if they think their bodies may be welcomed (*We had over 100 people at our last church event!*) but their voices and perspectives are not.

If you've been stagnating in conflict, reflect and ask: Whose voices and whose perspectives have been evident in our church decisions? Whose voices and whose perspectives are missing? Find those missing voices. Welcome them. Value them. These are the voices that will make all the difference.

Reflection Questions

If your aim is to address an active conflict within your church, consider these questions:

1. How can the lens of cultural context help us view our conflict differently?

2. Consider the questions posed in the text of this chapter. Whose voices and whose perspectives have been evident in our church decisions? Whose voices and whose perspectives are missing?

3. What are some ways we can show those whose voices have been missing that we are serious about valuing them in this process?

If your aim is to proactively outfit your church with healthy conflict-resolution skills, consider these questions:

1. Are there different cultural backgrounds represented in our church? If so, what are they?

2. How does our church view cultural differences?

3. How could we use the information in this chapter to give our congregation members more resources for resolving conflict?

4. What stands out to you in this chapter? What do you notice?

Notes

Roles

As we mentioned in the introduction, there are many reasons why you might have picked up this book. You may be somebody who feels embroiled in a church tension, and you want to stop the argument from negatively impacting your relationships.

Maybe you are a clergy member who sees a conflict emerging amongst your membership, and you want to set your congregation up for success. You might also be searching for tools that your members could use to resolve the current issue and lay a foundation for healthy conflict transformation in the future. There are many different motivations for engaging in this work. However, the ultimate goal of this material is healthy conflict transformation, and the curriculum requires several roles to be successful. These roles include Facilitator, Clergy, Church Leaders, Host, Planning Team, and Congregation.

Facilitator

The modules require someone to shepherd participants through the various activities, and that responsibility falls on the person we define as the facilitator. The facilitator is crucial to the success of this process. Although this role could be shared among two or three people, we'll be talking about it here as just one role. The person in this role should be able to hold onto the big picture of the work you'll be doing together. Prior to planning or inviting people into the decision-making space, they should read and understand the entire arc of the process that is laid out in the modules we've provided. We strongly suggest that the pastor of the congregation working through these modules and the facilitator be two different people. (We discuss the role of pastor below.) However, this is not to say that the facilitator role can't or shouldn't be filled by a pastor. We only recommend a pastor filling the facilitator role should have little or no personal connection to the congregation undergoing the process, as this could create a power dynamic that could hurt or even derail the *Calm* process.

The role of the facilitator is to be a neutral party. This person will lead the group, whether in person or virtually, and offer a sense of trust and safety to the process by guiding the group through the curriculum in a fluid manner. When choosing a facilitator, you want to select someone who can lead unbiasedly. They should not be someone who has a stake in any particular outcome, but should be fair to those on all sides of the issue. This person must also possess high emotional intelligence, which, according to the Harvard Business School definition, means "the ability to understand and manage your own emotions, as well as recognize and influence the emotions of those around you."[3]

In this role, the goal isn't to influence others regarding the outcome of the resolution but, instead, the facilitator will influence the process by paying close attention to who is speaking too much and who hasn't spoken at all, or by recognizing when the participants need a break. The facilitator must be able to read the mood of the room and remain calm during heated conversations.

A good facilitator is able to hold multiple perspectives at once, without pushing a discussion toward one idea or the other. They need to prioritize the process over any one particular destination. As group members share their thoughts, the facilitator's role will often be to help model what it looks like to hold space for those hopes and fears. They should ask for clarity where people are having difficulty being understood, and for less speaking from those who would take up the entire discussion. It is a role that requires someone who is able to sit in the discomfort of setting and holding boundaries.

For this work to succeed, all of the participants must feel that the process values their voices and that they are respected. It is the facilitator's role to

---

3. Lauren Landry, "Why Emotional Intelligence Is Important in Leadership," https://online.hbs.edu/blog/post/emotional-intelligence-in-leadership.

ardently model respect of everyone's dignity—the kind and courteous participant and the grumpy combative participant.

Imagine that you are in an argument with someone, and you meet with an authority figure to help you resolve your issue. How would you feel if that teacher, boss, or person in a position of power makes a decision without respecting your opinion? In that situation, you likely won't feel comforted. Instead, you might feel more anger and resentment. Facilitators help to de-escalate conflict by offering a trusted guide through the curriculum that encourages participation from all.

There might be someone within your congregation who can take on this role for your process. However, you may need to search outside your membership for an appropriate person. Consider asking your district superintendent for potential candidates. Similarly, your conference leadership may know of a resource, or you can ask a clergy member from a nearby congregation to lead the curriculum.

Throughout the modules, we have included specific tips and reminders for the group facilitator. We offer these after many years of leading groups of various sizes, backgrounds, and settings.

Tips for facilitating this material:

- Be prepared: know the curriculum inside and out.
- Balance the conversation amongst the participants.
- Ask follow-up questions to clarify what participants mean if it is unclear.
- Anticipate the needs of the group.
- Encourage the group to remember the established boundaries.

Clergy

The next role that is critical to the success of the curriculum is that of the clergy member. *Calm* is intentionally designed to be led by church members. However, your clergy person plays an important and integral role in ensuring the church is healthy and managing conflict well.

In times of internal struggle, church members often turn to their pastor for support, which sometimes forces that clergy person to become an ultimate arbitrator. This material, however, asks clergy to be a part of the process, not the leader. The curriculum intentionally levels the power dynamic between all of the participants and views everyone as critical team members in resolving the issue and imagining a healthy path forward.

Congregations often look first to their pastor or clergy staff for leadership. That is a vocation and a calling that the pastors we've worked with have taken very seriously. It's important in this decision-making process for the pastor to be clear in their support of this process.

It's not uncommon for people to put their pastor on a pedestal and default to the choice the pastor suggests. On the one hand, you may find people who disagree with a decision are more likely to simply stop participating or change churches, than to consider speaking up or to suggest an alternative plan. On the other hand, there are others who will engage in a kind of lobbying of their idea and undermine the choice they disagree with. In both circumstances, you find people who feel unheard. A thriving, forward-moving community is built within spaces that value all voices and provide opportunities for sharing contrasting ideas, with healthy boundaries in place to prevent harm.

The best support the pastor can offer to this process is to remain an active listener, so as not to stifle sharing from the group members or add to the conflict by unintentionally joining one side of the discussion.

If you are a clergy member, then the idea of handing over the leadership of this process may feel like a relief or a threat. You may welcome the support of more participants in the process and want your congregation members to take greater authority in resolving conflicts. But let's acknowledge that can also be difficult. If you are a pastor reading this, we know that you have strong convictions and beliefs in what is right and wrong. You have vision and hope for the future of your congregants, your local church, and even the church in general. And you may find yourself in the midst of a conflict where you have very strong convictions. The challenge to you in this process is to hold those convictions, to allow yourself to sit in the potential discomfort of not taking the reins. Even if it feels uncomfortable to be an equal participant, remember that in doing so you can take off your "church leader" hat and truly engage in the work.

As the clergy person, you will set the tone. Modeling faithful and joyful servant-leadership in this process will signify to the participants that it is okay for them to be vulnerable as well. Additionally, your trust in the facilitator will help the group to accept the facilitator's part in the curriculum.

The clergy member's role will include planning for the events, inviting the congregation to join, and meeting with the facilitator before the first module to offer your insight on how the conflict shows up within your faith community.

Tips for clergy members:

- Support the process with a glad heart.
- Sit back and relax.
- Pay close attention to how much you speak; create space for others.
- Be an advocate for the facilitator.

Church Leaders

Church leaders are persons who head your church's policy governance board or pastor-parish relationship committee. Church leaders may include the lay speakers in your congregation or even church staff. Church leaders will participate in the process but will also carry out the tasks of preparing for the events.

The role of a church leader in relationship to this curriculum is to model excitement about working through the conflict in a healthy manner that leads to stronger relationships and collaboration. In thousands of tiny ways, church leaders will signal to the congregation whether or not this process will be a success.

If you are a church leader, think of your job as one of a cheerleader or social media influencer. You will model a commitment to the process so that others will be motivated to participate in this curriculum as well. Your support of the work will encourage others to show up and commit to the hard work of addressing conflict in order to resolve it.

The church leader's voice will be crucial in inviting congregation members to the events. It may be helpful to ask church leaders to promote the process in a worship moment or to have informal conversations with their friends about the importance of the work and why they will participate.

Tips for church leaders:

- Reflect on why you feel this work is important so that you can articulate your perspective with others.

- Seek out church members who may avoid the process and offer a personal invitation.

- Model a commitment to the established boundaries.

- Engage in the work so that others will follow your example.

Host

Another role is that of the host. This should be a position that is easy to fill. United Methodists are good at setting up dessert tables with plates of cakes, cookies, and punch. We're good at doing coffee hour, Lenten dinners, and finding ways to connect with one another. Hosts play an important role in this work because, let's face it, conflict is hard! Critical conversations are taxing, and the host will help participants to feel comfortable.

Hosts will ensure that the doors are open, the space is set up, and the necessary materials are available for the various activities. The host will work hand in hand with the facilitator and will need to be aware of the curriculum beforehand so that they can prepare the space.

But most importantly, the host will be the friendly face, welcoming participants to the process. This position is not only for the in-person application of this curriculum. Think about all of the times that you've been invited to a Zoom meeting and you don't know where to locate the correct link or how to RSVP.

If you are a host engaging with this curriculum in the virtual format, you will ensure that everybody has the right links in order to attend the session, and you will show up early to open the virtual meeting and to admit participants into the room. You will also be the person that the facilitator will lean on to handle logistics during the modules so that they can focus on leading the activities. For instance, you will monitor the waiting room during the session in case people log off and need to re-enter. Additionally, you will offer technical assistance to those who may experience connectivity issues.

The host offers a smiling face while participants enter the virtual room to help avoid the awkward downtime before the process begins. Lastly, in this format that the host will work with the facilitator to add activity links into the chat or split the group into breakout rooms.

Tips for hosts:

- Acquaint yourself with common Zoom tech issues and solutions.
- Gather a team to set up the physical space if necessary.
- Consider whether or not you want to offer food, and if so, coordinate who will provide what items.

Planning Team

When preparing for this curriculum you will need to recruit a committee—something all United Methodists are good at doing! One thing that is helpful when you first gather your planning committee is to outline who is going to play what role. You will identify those individuals who will play the various roles of facilitator, host, and clergy person. You will also select church leaders with an intentional focus on those individuals who can encourage church members to participate.

Outlining what each person will be doing in regards to the curriculum offers clarity and ensures that tasks are covered but not duplicated. It is important to include members on both sides of your conflict in the planning team. Early collaboration will encourage other church members to take the process seriously and feel comfortable participating.

Tips for planning teams:

- Give yourself enough time to plan your events.
- Be clear on your vision.
- Define how you will recruit participants and what narratives you will use.
- Consider your church's calendar when scheduling dates for your events so you don't force participants to choose where they will spend their time.

The Congregation

Finally, we come to the role of the church body, which is the most important role in the entire process. We cannot stress this fact enough: in order to be successful, the congregation must be in the driver's seat of this process. This curriculum is intentionally led by the body of the church because that is a critical component to change management, and conflict resolution requires change. Imagine a church that receives a directive from their district or conference that they must make a change. If that church doesn't like the decision but has no say over the process, then those church members may feel resentful. *Voila*: conflict!

You may reflect on times that the denomination made decisions that have impacted your church. If members in your congregation didn't feel like they had a say in those decisions, and disagreed in the decision, it was likely hard to show your support. Therefore, it is critical that all voices around the issue are represented so that everyone will feel as though they were a part of the final solution. That is why this curriculum focuses on drawing out the voice of every single person who is around the physical table or the virtual Zoom room so that everyone feels like they have the opportunity to have their voice heard.

Tips for the congregation:

- Show up with an open mind and caring heart.
- Commit to being present, being honest, and showing love.
- Consider the lenses and frameworks you bring to the table, as well as any biases you may have. (And don't worry, all of us have biases, whether we acknowledge them or not.)

Navigating Change

Many conflicts are rooted in change. In fact, the two examples that we used when creating this material were conflicts related to change on a small scale and change on a large scale. We continually checked the usefulness of the curriculum's modules and activities against the scenarios of a church starting a new contemporary worship service as well as a church determining their next steps in the middle of a denominational schism. Both of the above examples represent changes for the church members that are tricky to manage. The good news is that there is a lot of research on initiating changes for organizations. One of our favorite frameworks for navigating change was created by John P. Kotter, the author of *Leading Change*. In his framework, Kotter outlines eight steps:

1. Create a Sense of Urgency

2. Build a Guiding Coalition

3. Form a Strategic Vision

4. Enlist a Volunteer Army

5. Enable Action by Removing Barriers

6. Generate Short-Term Wins

7. Sustain Acceleration

8. Institute Change

Two of the steps in his framework talk about the importance of engaging several individuals in the process. Even if you are the most passionate advocate for a change, if you do not enlist others in the process, alone you won't succeed. So essentially, even if you are the pastor of your congregation and you want your church to resolve a conflict healthily, you will not be able to force it to happen.

There are several ways you will relate to Kotter's framework when engaging in our curriculum. You must create a sense of urgency so others understand the importance of addressing the conflict. You then must pull together a planning team or guiding coalition to champion support for the process. Additionally, a clear vision of why the curriculum will benefit your church and church members is necessary to recruit participants.

Imagine you approached a church member and invited them to participate in the conflict-resolution process. An example of a strategic vision relating to our curriculum is the difference between saying, "Aren't you sick of fighting about the new bulletins?" and "Let's try our best to learn from one another and create a shared solution." Or, if someone asked you, "What are these events about? Why should I attend?" Instead of complaining about all the bickering between church members, you might say, "You should come because these events are focused on working through tough issues collectively, and your voice on the matter is important for others to hear."

The fourth step in Kotter's framework highlights the critical need for parties on both sides of the presenting issue to participate and claim ownership over the result. Your conflict will be resolved more effectively with the help of others. Not only will you need all the roles above to conduct the modules, but you will also need church members across the issue to attend and commit to the process.

Wearing Different Hats

As you read through the different roles that our curriculum requires, you probably reflected on how you might relate to the material. Did you see yourself as a part of the planning team? Would you like to facilitate the curriculum? Or, is it important for you to simply participate in the process because you want to share your thoughts and perspectives? Another thing to consider when leading this curriculum and thinking about the role that you will play is that no one has a single identity. No one is just a facilitator, just a clergy member, just a church leader.

Everyone has a myriad of ways that they relate to their church. You may be a participant in this process and on a committee at your church or a conference or district committee. No matter what the scenario may be, as a participant in this process, you will have ways that you will relate to the curriculum through the lens of your work and family life. Everyone brings multiple viewpoints to this process.

For example, imagine your church recently merged with another church nearby. Your two congregations may find themselves arguing over which building to use and which to sell or re-purpose. In this imagined scenario, if your church's conflict is around your building use and assets and you are a realtor, you would relate to the conversation in two different ways. Due to your profession, other participants may look to you to share guidance on real estate in your community. At the same time, you're likely to also have a personal opinion over which building is best, considering the fact that you grew up in your church.

Another illustration is if your church is debating whether to allocate funds for a children and family coordinator, and you are called upon to share your thoughts on budget realities because you serve on the finance committee. While you hold this leadership role in your congregation with the important task of maintaining the financial health of your church, you also might be a parent with high hopes for the program offerings available to your kids. The reality is that almost never are we able to look at an issue or conflict through a single lens.

This curriculum recognizes all the various ways that we relate to our church, the conflict, and the work of resolution. In fact, reflecting on your individual identity and creating a shared identity with other participants is the focus of the first module. It is essential to recognize that even individual participants may hold conflicting viewpoints. Reflecting on the many ways that we relate to the issue gives us insight on why we might be feeling tension.

Your Church's Unique Situation

Just as you relate to this work in many ways, your church is similarly complex. The conflict that is bubbling between your members might be impacted by several factors. This is because there are several individuals involved in your congregation and various internal factors—how many people you have on staff, the age of your congregation, or the traditions you've developed. Additionally, many external factors impact conflict-resolution work.

Conflicts are often focused on one symptom when really several complications and layers are involved. Think of a post-pandemic church whose members are fighting over whether or not to continue their traditional spaghetti dinner. For some, the event represents a return to business as usual. They remember laughing over salad and breadsticks each year and raising funds to support the youth mission trip. Opponents to the spaghetti dinner might be frustrated because there aren't enough volunteers to run the event. They feel pressured and overextended. Both sides may be focusing on the spaghetti dinner, but really they are grieving a church that is trying to claw itself back from a pandemic and adjust to the general church decline.

When you prepare to lead this material, your planning committee needs to consider the root cause of the conflict and the internal and external forces at play. Don't worry, though, if the root cause of your conflict is hard to identify. This is actually the norm. The modules we present are designed to dive deep into the tension you are experiencing and uncover deeper meaning.

No two churches and conflicts will have the same set of circumstances. Luckily, this curriculum offers the tools necessary to engage in healthy conversations. The material is available for you to use whenever conflicts arise. Though you may have purchased this book for one issue, once you have the tools for healthy conflict transformation, you can return to the process time and time again.

Reflection Questions

If your aim is to address an active conflict within your church, consider these questions:

1. What is the issue that is causing tension amongst our church members?

2. How does the tension show up in the daily life of our church?

3. What support do I need to implement this process?

4. What is my first step?

If your aim is to proactively outfit your church with healthy conflict-resolution skills, consider these questions:

1. How is conflict typically resolved in our congregation?

2. How might this process help us to address conflict in a healthy manner?

3. How could we use this information to give our congregation members more resources for resolving conflict?

4. What stands out to you in this chapter? What do you notice?

Notes

Dealing with Difficult Feelings and Loss

We are very aware of the context of the world in which we write this book. The circumstances of the worldwide pandemic have been incredibly draining for many groups of people. Our ability to connect with others changed overnight. How and where we work changed. Many people lost jobs or faced the choice of safety versus paying the bills. The health of ourselves and our loved ones was at stake; our routines and lifestyles were altered. Not only have we lived through a Covid-19 pandemic, but also there has been job and housing insecurity, racial unrest, political abuse and division, and violence. Collectively, we have been through a traumatic period, and many are left mentally and emotionally exhausted.

People's ability to tolerate change and to navigate and regulate themselves through conflict may be lower than in the past. As a facilitator or supporter of this process, it will be helpful to know how people's feelings may be revealed in their behaviors through this process. You may also find it helpful to consider your own reactions to experiences of loss, which may be stirred up during this process. Having this insight will also help you maintain boundaries so that the expression of feelings remains an open part of the process, without harming others.

Internalizing and Externalizing Behaviors

Participants in your group are likely to respond to difficult feelings through either internalizing or externalizing behaviors. Both serve the purpose of providing a sense of control when a person is beginning to feel powerless. Often, having these behaviors named aloud in a compassionate way can be enough to help a person walk through the discomfort without disengaging.

Internalizing behaviors are, as you might imagine, directed inward toward oneself. You might notice someone beginning to shut down, participate less, or retreat to another area of the room. They may share thoughts of self-doubt or express physical discomforts, like an upset stomach or headache. Internalizing behaviors can be difficult for someone else to see, which is why it's important for facilitators to normalize taking breaks or to provide ways for people to engage in self-care throughout the process.

In contrast, externalizing behaviors are presented outward and often are the most triggering for others. Examples may include confrontational or argumentative speech, denial of the circumstances, bargaining or crying, or becoming hyper-focused on getting small "wins." These kinds of externalized behaviors can feel wounding to others in the group. For the facilitator, it's helpful to hold the mind-set that these behaviors are a reaction to a person's own inner discomfort and to help name the emotion behind the behavior. For example, people should be allowed to express that they feel angry, but they should not be allowed to belittle or silence others.

Understanding your own tendency to internalize or externalize during discomfort, as well as doing the inner work of learning how to recognize and regulate yourself during those moments, is crucial to supporting others through this process. As previously discussed, a facilitator's role is to uphold each person's dignity and inclusion in this process, while de-escalating conflict when necessary, which requires a person capable of self-regulation.

Grief and Loss

You may wonder why we're dedicating a section in a book about conflict and change to discussing the basics of grief and loss. Our clinical and professional experience has taught us that these two areas are indelibly linked. The same emotions and coping strategies that we experience during the loss of a loved one can arise in us during the loss of a routine or tradition. That's not to say that a building or object carries the same inherent worth as a human being, but rather that how we emotionally process changes and losses happens in similar patterns.

That said, it's important to note that this is not a clinical textbook, and what we are offering is intended to ground you in preparation for this specific work but therefore cannot be fully comprehensive. While the patterns and behaviors below provide a helpful overview, how grief manifests in each person is unique. A person who has experienced many losses, but processed them well, may react very differently than a person who has experienced only one major loss but experienced complicated grief, such as might happen in a highly traumatic event.

The Stages of Grief

In the late 1960s, psychiatrist Elisabeth Kübler-Ross authored the now-famous theory of the five stages of grief. In our experience and context, it's best to understand these stages not as a linear process, where you leave one stage to move into the next like stair steps, but rather as co-existing spheres, where you might move through a range of stages at any given time. Understanding these spheres or stages will help you recognize if and when a related response shows up in your group.

First, it's critical to understand that each stage of grief is our body's or brain's way of trying to help us cope. It is purposeful, even if not always rational. In the context of change management, we might find that our brain's first go-to coping patterns aren't helpful. Maintaining a curious and reflective attitude is important to help get past those patterns and return to being present in the moment.

Denial

Denial is our brain's way of slowing down the amount of information we're taking in and helping us cope with overwhelming negative feelings, such as fear or sadness. This may look like refusing to face inevitable change or attempting to ignore or normalize current problems.

Denial is rooted in a fear of loss.

During this process, denial will commonly present as people saying they want to "go back to the way things were" despite the reality that time can only ever move forward. People stuck in denial want to avoid conflict by refusing to hear more than they think they can handle. Naming and acknowledging the conflict is often the simplest way to help them move forward.

Anger

Anger, as it relates to grief or loss, is our body's way of protecting us from fear, judgment, and rejection. It provides a way for us to engage without having to sit with those feelings that make us uncomfortable.

During this process, you may see people expressing frustration at the whole process, and they may have a confrontational or argumentative tone of voice with others. This might result in them feeling isolated or abandoned when others avoid talking with them. Anger can be expressed both externally and internally. You may notice people become resentful or disengaged, expressing things like "why bother" or "no one wants to listen to me anyway."

Facilitators who notice anger coming out this way should try to remain nonjudgmental and not meet confrontation with confrontation. Instead, reflect back what you're noticing in the person's behavior and hold them responsible for upholding the group boundaries. For example, if a group member gets heated and calls another person's idea stupid or wrong, the facilitator might say, "You seem to be feeling really angry right now, and we can hold space for everyone's feelings through this process. But we've also agreed as a group not to attack or demean anyone's ideas. How would you like to proceed?" This puts the responsibility back on the individual person but also upholds the safety of the group. Additionally, it allows for the facilitator to pivot, if the group member is not able to manage their anger, and to offer a specific suggestion such as taking a short break.

Guilt or Bargaining

Guilt or bargaining is our brain's way of trying to regain control when we feel powerless. This could look like a person ruminating on the past and things they wish they had done. Similar to denial, this is a way of avoiding the current reality by focusing on things like, "If only we had done this or that . . ." It could also present as someone putting unreasonable expectations on themselves for the future. Others in this stage may feel guilty sharing conflicting opinions with others, feeling somehow responsible for others' feelings and fearing a potential loss of connection.

This is an opportunity to emphasize that this process is about working together in community. Today's challenges are not because of anything one person did or didn't do, and the way forward won't be up to only one person either.

A complicated way that bargaining may present itself during this process is through the act of prayer. In our faith tradition as United Methodists, we believe that prayer is a heartfelt, necessary component in the life of the church, and we would never discourage it. But for some, it can become an expression of coping via "bargaining" with God. Consider the common parable of a man telling passing lifeboats that he's waiting for God to rescue him from flood waters. As people of faith, we trust in God and pray for discernment, but we also recognize our responsibility to have hard conversations, trust each other, and show up through action.

Lastly, guilt and bargaining should not be confused for healthy, appropriate feelings of repentance or remorse. When people hear new perspectives, they often look back at things they've said or done and feel apologetic or regretful. That is a healthy part of social development and a sign that you have created a nurturing, brave space where people are deepening their compassion for one another.

Sadness or Depression

The next area is sadness or depression. During this response, our brains and our bodies are recognizing the reality of our circumstances. This is when our loss feels very present and unavoidable.

At points in this process, you may notice some people seeking time alone or appearing to feel overwhelmed. Some people may cry or show their sadness in their body language. A person might speak or think more slowly than is typical or seem less productive.

Consider having specific breaks planned or discussing together if the group is willing to take a break whenever someone requests. Remember that it's important to allow space for a full range of feelings. We want to allow people to have the space they need to process and honor what they may be saying good-bye to. Sadness is often an indicator that a person is not avoiding what feels hard, which means they may actually be more able to face conflict and move forward.

Acceptance

The last of the five stages of grief and loss is acceptance, which is our way of reconciling with our feelings and finding meaning from our experience. Acceptance does not mean a person is no longer affected by the loss. But rather it means that they have found a way to incorporate that loss into their lives and move forward.

During this process, for example, a person may choose to cut ties with a church after it disaffiliates but find meaning in connections they've made with other advocates. Or a person may accept that a favorite service or beloved tradition will no longer be part of their church moving forward. It doesn't mean they no longer care about those past experiences or that they didn't feel deeply impacted. By allowing them to share their story and to be heard by others, we help people to find acceptance.

Even with acceptance, we shouldn't assume that people are unbothered or "over it," which is why it is still important to name and hold space for feelings of loss, even if those feelings go unspoken. We've included a module dedicated to honoring this part of the process, acknowledging that feelings of hope, joy, and renewal can exist alongside feelings of fear, uncertainty, and grief.

Recognizing and holding space for grief and loss doesn't mean we have to stay stuck. The feelings that come up aren't excuses for treating others poorly, either. But staying curious and compassionate helps keep us in healthy community with one another and honors our sacred worth as children of God.

Seeing through Her Eyes: An Example of Understanding through a Context of Loss

We keep all these things in mind, not only because we wish to know one another better and to help one another through hard times, but also because they play a real role in how decisions get made and in people's motivations in how they talk about different ideas. We hold them in mind because of stories like this.

Linda was an older woman who had attended a particular downtown United Methodist church for as long as anyone could remember. She had been there before the current pastor and the pastors before that. She always sat in the same seat, in the same pew, and people commonly knew it was her spot. She was someone you could count on.

There came a time when the church leadership wanted to create a space in the sanctuary for young children and their parents to sit, to quietly play, and to be part of the worshipping community. The children's director had seen similar spaces at other churches and was passionate about creating a welcoming space for families. They would remove three sections of pews on one side and create their "prayground."

Linda had a long history of supporting ministries for children and families. She'd raised her own children in the church, had volunteered at vacation bible school and in the nursery, and contributed to youth fundraisers. She loved seeing the babies and didn't seem to mind when they cried or made noise during the service. Church leaders were surprised when they learned that Linda was complaining about the new plans to create a family space in the sanctuary. They expected the kind of support she'd always offered in the past.

The children's director thought to "test the waters" and approached Linda one Sunday morning. They shared a little about their weeks and some upcoming events, and the children's director said she's looking forward to growing their family program. Linda nodded in agreement. Feeling encouraged, the children's director mentioned that perhaps new mothers would like to be able to sit in a rocker during worship, rather than having to go to the nursery. She noticed that Linda's face got a little tight, but she continued to outline her ideas and how she had seen success at other churches. But Linda remained resistant, and the director left feeling discouraged and confused.

Sometimes when we look forward, we can forget to honor the rich experiences of others. We can miss opportunities to build bridges because we jump to a conclusion rather than remain curious. This kind of interpersonal conflict happens often in churches, and it's why we strongly encourage people to practice the kind of community-building we talk about in this book. Not just when a single, big decision is being made, but with the small relationship repairs that help sustain healthy communities.

Applying a curious lens, we would learn that Linda had indeed been attending this same church for years, as a child, a teen, and an adult. She had sat in that same spot with her parents, with her children and husband, and with her grandchildren when they visited. From that seat, right of the center aisle, three rows back, she had taken in countless verses of scripture. For years, she'd watched light enter the sanctuary through the same stained-glass window, experienced changing seasons, and watched the light move across the altar year after year. All from the same place. It was where she sat with her husband before he passed, and where she remembered him and their family together.

Some of the most deeply holy, sacred moments in Linda's life happened right here, week after week, year after year.

Using a lens of grief and loss, we can begin to understand what Linda's experience has meant to her and how it has shaped her into a leader in their church. Through understanding and compassion, Linda's experience was honored and held and she was invited to share what the church has meant to her through these years and to be part of dedicating that space to future parents and caregivers. Honoring another person's experience doesn't mean that we remain frozen in time or never make changes to our spaces. But it can lead to a richer experience and deeper connection as we move forward together.

Reflection Questions

If your aim is to address an active conflict within your church, consider these questions:

1. Do you notice the stages of grief arising in your conflict?

2. What can you do to share this information with your team?

3. How can your team use this lens to support your conflict-resolution work?

4. What stage(s) resonates with you as you consider your church's conflict?

If your aim is to proactively outfit your church with healthy conflict-resolution skills, consider these questions:

1. Can you think of a time when these stages have presented themselves in your congregation?

2. How might this lens of understanding support your church's future conflict-resolution work?

3. Which church groups could you share this chapter with to lay the groundwork for understanding conflict?

4. What stands out to you in this chapter? What do you notice?

Notes

Preparing to Lead

A key component to facilitating these modules is the ability to stay regulated in your own emotions, which can be difficult when you're discussing challenging issues that people care deeply about. Preparing your physical space and materials will help you, in the long run, to feel calmer and more settled as you navigate tense or emotional moments. It's key to remember that preparation is never about thinking of every possible scenario that could occur. That's an impossible task. But having a roadmap in your minds as leaders will allow you to feel comfortable adjusting and being flexible within your larger plan. When you are prepared, you are more capable of pivoting when the unexpected or the inspired happens. That skill is crucial since each group will find meaning through the modules in unique and rich ways.

As you work through these initial planning stages, keep in mind that the most successful experiences begin with relationships. Recruit potential facilitators or volunteers by sharing the strengths they will bring to the process. Make authentic personal invitations to members of the congregation or key stakeholders, letting them know that their voice and perspective are valuable in this process. Be willing to listen to the concerns that people bring you about past group experiences that may have left them feeling discouraged. Be honest about your commitment to bringing various viewpoints together, which may sometimes feel uncomfortable. Don't make any false promises about any particular outcome, but name your commitment to holding a safe space for their voice to be heard.

If you choose to use these modules in a virtual or hybrid setting, be sure to confirm that all participants have the access and knowledge to utilize the online video platform. It might be helpful to add an additional meeting time prior to Module One to review the basics of the platform or any presenter tools, such as Mentimeter or Google Drive. Review how to mute or unmute and how to use various functions such as raising their hand, using reactions, using the chat or polls, and so on. Depending on your needs, you may also want to have some available technology for group members to borrow, such as webcams, laptops, or microphones.

Opening and Closing Routine

Create a simple opening and closing ritual for yourselves as facilitators and leaders, such as praying together or doing a short mindfulness activity or a breath activity. Set this time aside intentionally as a way of centering and grounding yourselves before the work of the day, and again as a way of honoring the work that was done and marking the end of the day. In our experience, it's not uncommon for group leaders to gather together before a session but then drift away at the end of the meeting. We encourage you not to drift, but to be intentional and take a moment together after the session has finished. This could look like circling together and offering a single word that you're taking with you from the day. Or it could be a quiet moment of gratitude to God and one another.

Closing routines or rituals help our brains to process information and allow us to make transitions from one activity to the next. By having a consistent, predictable moment to close, you're allowing your brain to flip that switch off, knowing you'll be able to switch it back on for the next module. These routines create healthy mental and emotional boundaries around the work. They are a reminder that this process is not all on your shoulders, but is the collective responsibility of the community. When the community gathers, be present and rested and ready to lead. And when it's time to step away, allow yourself the gift of not carrying everything with you.

Supporting Group Wellness

Each community or group that you bring together for this work is inherently comprised of individual people with individual needs and learning styles. We have worked to provide a variety of activities that will provide a rich experience for extroverts or introverts, visual learners or kinesthetic learners, and more. You can support that experience even further by making wellness resources and tools available that meet diverse needs. For example, research has shown that using fidget items may help people self-regulate to boost attention or increase calm. Doodling or coloring can help to slow racing thoughts or can be used as a coping strategy for difficult emotions. These items could be located at a specific table within the meeting space or placed among the small-group tables. We've included a list of suggestions below. If meeting virtually, consider creating individual bags with a few different supplies for people to have at home.

Getting Started—Checklists

The remainder of this chapter is information that can be found in other parts of the book and the modules. We've put that information here in a collection of lists to help you organize yourself to begin. Use the extra spaces provided to add whatever you need for your particular setting.

Leadership Choices:

- Identify who will take on the roles outlined in this chapter (facilitator, clergy, church leaders, host, planning team) and share this resource with them.

- Review material with the assembled team and discuss any questions or ideas together as a group.

- Decide if you will use an in-person, virtual, or hybrid style.

- Determine meeting space for each of the modules, if in person or hybrid.

    o Consider using one space for Modules One through Three.

    o Consider meeting in your church's sanctuary or chapel space for Module Four.

- o Consider using a different space for Module Five to accommodate more participants and circle seating. Also, consider providing small-group workspaces, such as church classrooms, various tables, or outdoor spaces (if appropriate).

- Recruit a music leader or have recorded music for worship in Module Four and optional closing song in Module Three.

- Send invites to potential participants or congregation.

Setup Needed:

- Tables and chairs for participants
- Microphone for leaders (as needed)
- Speakers to play music
- Video projector, screen, and computer and any adapters/cords needed to connect them
- Blank wall space to hang various displays or posters
- Meal tables (Module Five, optional)

Supplies Needed:

- Name tags
- Markers
- Pens/Pencils
- Poster paper or whiteboards
- Lined or unlined paper for note-taking and various activities
- Calm music and video/photo imagery
- Selected images for "Seeing from Other Perspectives" (Module One)
- Selected images for "Describe, Interpret, Evaluate" (Module Two); multiple copies, if desired
- Tape or wall putty to hang poster papers on walls
- Sticky notes: four different colors; enough for each table to have a stack of all four colors (such as pink, green, yellow, orange)
- Copies of Heppenstall closing prayer (Module One, optional)
- Display materials to represent the work of the group (Module Three)
- Copy of prayer for collective decision-making (Module Three)
- Ranked-choice voting materials (Module Three)
- Prayer walk materials (Module Three)
- Copy of closing song or benediction (Module Three)
- Worship materials (Module Four)
  - *United Methodist Hymnal, Faith We Sing,* and/or *Worship & Song*
  - Candle and match/lighter (or battery-operated candle)
  - Alter or table to place candle
  - Images: nature/moving air; closed and open hands
  - Copies of worship outline for leaders and participants, as needed
  - Copies of music or lyrics
- Worksheet for S.M.A.R.T. goals (Module Five, optional)

Self-Care and Wellness Suggestions:

- Fidget items (stretchy sensory strings, stress balls, puffer balls)
- Breathing exercises
- Stress-less cards (available from Amazon or other retailers)
- Art or doodle materials (mandalas, colored pencils, sticky notes, play-doh, putty)
- Visual sensory items (glitter wands, liquid motion bubblers)
- Unscented lotion
- Healthy snacks (fruit, granola bars, protein snack packs)
- Water

Virtual-Specific Needs:

- Online meeting platform (such as Zoom)
- Access to a shared drive account (such as Google Docs, OneDrive)
- Access to Mentimeter (optional)
- Participants able to access a computer with video and audio capabilities in a private space
- Calming music and imagery video or photos with music
- Ranked-choice voting materials such as Google Forms (Module Three)
- Virtual prayer walk materials (Module Three)

Reflection Questions

If your aim is to address an active conflict within your church, consider these questions:

1. What opening and closing routine could your planning team use?
2. Does your church already use techniques and tools for supporting group wellness as listed above, or are those new concepts?
3. What tools and materials does your church have, and what might you need to collect?
4. What is your first step?

If your aim is to proactively outfit your church with healthy conflict resolution skills, consider these questions:

1. How might the group wellness supportive tools and suggestions help your church's current programs?
2. Are there ways that you already engage in opening and closing routines?
3. What materials and supplies might your church need to collect in order to support a process like the one offered in this text?
4. What stands out to you in this chapter? What do you notice?

Notes

Modules

Now that you have read through the preceding chapters on the context of this material, it is time to dive into the curriculum. We devoted the remainder of this book to the modules: how to lead them, what supplies and tools are needed, and what activities are included. Think of this material as a leader or facilitator guide and consider how you might use it with your congregation.

Module One: Acknowledging the Struggle

Module One will take approximately three hours.

And let us consider how we may spur one another on toward love and good deeds, not giving up meeting together, as some are in the habit of doing, but encouraging one another—and all the more as you see the Day approaching.
(Hebrews 10:24-25 NIV)

Our journey through conflict begins at Module One, where the main objective is to build an intentional community and create a sense of a shared group culture together. This first module names the issue at hand, so that participants are clear about what they will be working towards over the course of the process's five modules. But outside of clarifying the purpose of gathering at the beginning of the modules and defining a shared vision statement by the module's end, the conflict is not the focus of this first module. Some participants might find this a bit odd, or wonder, "Didn't we come here to resolve a conflict? Why aren't we talking about the conflict?"

But for this process ultimately to be successful, the participants need to trust one another deeply to feel safe enough to share in some potentially tough conversations. The group needs to become a cohesive unit. And it's not safe to assume that because you are all part of the same congregation, or consider yourselves a church family, that you will function through this process as a unit. And it's not safe to assume that a deep level of trust exists. If we're completely honest, we know our church families are not quite as cohesive as they may seem on the outside, and this is true of the church's leaders too.

Church leaders may meet together weekly and work cooperatively on all sorts of ministries, but the process they're about to go through will expose hidden differences. You need to be ready for that.

So, the first priority is community-building. This is best done through group activities that, though they may seem low-stakes or even a bit frivolous on the surface, actually serve a much higher purpose. We are breaking down walls and building trust, laying the foundation for the work to follow.

Gathering & Setup | Prior to Start

Participants will gather for Module One within an inviting meeting space. Facilitator(s) will greet participants as they arrive. Set up enough tables and chairs for the expected number of participants. There must be enough space for large group activities to take place in the front of the room, as well as space to break up into small working groups when instructed. We recommend providing name tags and setting out light refreshments to help create a welcoming atmosphere.

Virtual Adaptation: Participants join a virtual meeting space where calming music and video/photo imagery is playing as they gather.

Introducing *Calm* | 10 minutes

Participants are welcomed by the facilitator(s), and the general intention of the gathering is named.

Say: *We have gathered today to find a way forward beyond the issue of _____. We will be using a curriculum found in the book* Calm: How to End Destructive Conflict in Your Church *to navigate this journey together. Today's session is the first in a series of five sessions, outlined in Modules One through Five in the book. We are so glad you have decided to journey alongside us through this process.*

Share the Mission Statement: Calm *offers churches the skills and tools necessary to engage in critical conversations that lead to healthy communities.*

Share the Theory of Change: *Churches that find themselves stuck in a cycle of conflict and division limit their abilities to fully live into Christ's holy community. Engaging in critical conversations with the intention of loving our neighbors, even when they disagree with us, allows churches to break cycles of conflict and free themselves to live into God's will for healthy communities.*

Say: *Ultimately the level of success we find together will rely on your willingness to live into this intention. We know we're here for a reason. We know we bring different perspectives and priorities. By engaging with one another, we can find a healthy way forward. Through intentional conversation and exploratory exercises, we will further unpack the problem, name potential solutions or options, and ultimately make a decision about what to do next. Let's begin!*

Virtual Adaptation: Along with the points above, a general introduction to the functions of the virtual platform should be given (camera on/camera off, mute mic, raise hand, and so on) to ensure all participants are comfortable utilizing the virtual platform. The facilitator(s) should also convey the following expectations that are necessary to build trust and community across a virtual space: Participants should plan to be using a computer (not a phone or a tablet) for ease of participating in the forthcoming activities, and because phones and tablets are easier to disengage from. Participants should be in a private space/place and keep their video on throughout the gathering time.

Establishing Boundaries | 15 minutes

So in Christ we, though many, form one body, and each member belongs to all the others. (Romans 12:5 NIV)

The goal of this first, whole-group exercise is to establish behavioral expectations for the duration of the curriculum. Having mutually agreed-upon boundaries is an important step in creating feelings of safety amongst the group. The *Calm* process is most effective when participants commit to being present and honest. You may say:

> *The first thing we need to do as we begin is to establish boundaries. During our time together, we may have heavy conversations. You may find yourself uncomfortable, and, quite simply, boundaries help us feel more safe as we participate in this process. Throughout the work today and in the days to come, these are the expectations to which we ask participants to hold themselves, and others, accountable:*
>
> ***Be Present:*** *Make the conscious decision to participate fully in the conversations and process. You are here for a reason and your point of view is incredibly important. "Phoning it in" behaviors directly conflict with the goal of the curriculum, which is to move through an issue to the healthy community that God calls us into.*
>
> ***Be Honest:*** *As Brené Brown says in Dare to Lead, "Clear is kind, unclear is unkind." Sharing your truth with honesty and respect is key to helping others to understand your point of view. Hiding feelings and avoiding behaviors perpetuate conflict.*
>
> ***Show Love:*** *We are called through faith to recognize the sacredness of each person in our group. Although we may not always agree or understand, we can choose to show love and respect in how we treat and speak to one another.*

Facilitators will unpack the meaning of each of these terms. Then, solicit input from the group through discussion or use of a virtual chat for other boundaries and expectations. Through the work of setting group boundaries and expectations together, the participants are beginning to create a shared culture and to build trust and a sense of safety among one another.

Virtual Adaptation: Facilitators should share their screen as they record boundaries and save to refer back to during later modules.

Participants may mention items like:

- Be present.

- Be honest.

- Show up on time.

- Share your feelings.

- Silence electronics.

- Keep confidentiality.

- Avoid posting on social media.

- Avoid "you" statements.

- Take breaks when they are needed.

- Show love.

- Use respectful language.

- Assume the best intent of others.

- Listen to other perspectives.

Breaking the Ice | 15 minutes

We present several options of potential icebreaker activities; your group need only do one. The purpose of all of these activities is simply to help the participants get to know one another a little better, through a light-hearted activity. Hopefully the activity will make participants smile and laugh, as laughing together is an important bonding activity. Choose an activity the members of your group will be able to do easily and comfortably; this is not yet the time to get folks to stretch much beyond their comfort zone.

Choose one option:

Two-Minute Statements: Invite participants to share two-minute statements about themselves. **Virtual Adaptation:** To help this move smoothly, facilitators may want to create a prompt or set of questions to share on the screen. (This option is best with a small group.)

Grab from the Kitchen: This is a quick and somewhat silly icebreaker, good for large groups in a virtual space. Ask participants to go to their kitchen and grab one piece of cutlery/silverware, but instruct them *not* to show it until you ask. (Most should return with either a spoon, knife, or fork.) When ready, ask for the big reveal and tally which cutlery type wins. This is a fun activity and also helps people move their bodies for about twenty to thirty seconds.

This or That: Invite group members to consider what their preferences are for a series of different scenarios. Some examples: Television series or movie? Delivery or sit-down restaurant? Board games or card games? Try to incorporate movement in order to collect responses. For example, participants can move to different places in the room to indicate their choice. In smaller places (or for virtual gatherings), people who choose "this" could put a hand on their forehead while those choose "that" could put a hand on their chin. **Virtual Adaptation:** Another option is to use the Zoom reactions, such as a thumbs up or a heart.

Common Ground: Allow the group to self-divide into pairs, though encourage them to work with someone they don't know very well. Give the pairs this prompt: "Relationships are built on shared experiences and a sense of community. As we aim to build relationships with each other, let's see what you can find in common." Allow the pairs roughly five minutes just to chat, to see what they can find in common with each other. Then, regroup and have each pair share their commonalities with the larger group. This activity can be repeated with new pairs, if time allows (but challenge the new pairs not to repeat commonalities).

Polls: Use Zoom polls or another site, such as mentimeter.com, to create several online polls for participants to answer. For example, "Which superpower would you like to have? (a) Mind reading; (b) Invisibility; (c) Teleportation; (d) Flying; (e) I already have a superpower." As responses are collected, share results with the group.

Word Clouds: Use a real-time word-cloud creator, such as mentimeter. com, to gather responses to simple, open-ended questions. For example, "What one thing would you take along with you to a desert island?" (Questions with one-word answers will typically work best.)

Building an Intentional Community

After setting boundaries and conducting a light-hearted icebreaker, group members will begin to feel more comfortable engaging with one another in general. This is of particular importance if utilizing a virtual space. The goal now is to begin to deepen an understanding of how to be in a healthy community with one another, while staying mindful of being present, being honest, and showing love.

Who Am I? | 40 minutes

Invite participants to number a piece of paper from 1-10 with space for responses to ten questions. When ready, the facilitator will ask ten consecutive times: "Who am I?" After everyone has finished, ask them to cross off three of the items. When ready, ask them to cross off three more items.

Facilitators will invite group members to process and reflect in small groups for in-person gatherings, or virtual breakout rooms:

- What types of responses did you write for your identity? (Some people may not be comfortable sharing all of their identity descriptors, which should be respected.)
- How did it feel to cross items off?
- What types of responses were crossed off first/last (that is, most negative, least important, and so on)?
- What can you learn from this activity about how you see yourself?

Virtual Adaptation: Before splitting to breakout rooms, facilitators will let participants know that they may be popping into the small groups throughout to observe and offer input. If no input is needed, facilitators will remain muted and move on to another group.

Breaking Down the Walls* | 15 minutes

*This activity may be deemed unnecessary for in-person groups.

For **virtual gatherings**, explain: *Trying to build community in a virtual space can feel very disconnecting and disorienting. We find ourselves simultaneously in two spaces—the square image on our* *computer screen and the physical space where we sit. The purpose of this activity is to help us mentally break through some of those walls, as well as engage and show some love to our bodies.*

Choose one or more:

Pass the Pen: Ask participants to get a pen or pencil, switch their Zoom view to gallery, and unmute themselves. Explain: "We're going to work together to 'pass the pen' around our whole group. I will begin by moving my pen across the screen and calling the name of someone else in the group. Then that person will 'receive' the pen, move it along their screen, and pass it to someone else. The goal is to 'pass the pen' to every person in the group. Let's begin! I'm going to pass the pen to Mary!"

Sound Ball: The goal is to throw around an invisible/imaginary ball to each person. Someone starts by forming and holding an invisible ball and saying the name of the person they're about to "throw" it to. The thrower has to make a specific sound with their mouth when throwing (such as "whee," "boing," "poof," "blah," or "shayayayaya"). The catcher must make the same sound that the thrower made, then name and throw to another person with a new made-up sound. Keep going until everyone has had the ball once. (Tip: Have everyone put their hands up to the camera if they haven't had the ball yet, so that as the game continues, the remaining throwers know who to throw to.)

High Fives: End by inviting everyone to air-high-five their neighbors, then air-high-five their diagonal neighbors!

Shake It Out: Play the "shake it out" video from Dr. Dana Maryse Shapero (TikTok: @simplybecome). After everyone has watched the video once, invite people to stand up and shake it out as the video plays again. **Virtual Adaptation:** Facilitators play the video through the screen share function. (Tip: Some people might feel more comfortable if they can turn off their video.)

Alternative: After watching once, invite everyone to "pass the shake" (think: doing the wave at a ball game). Invite one person to start, and as soon as you see your neighbor shake, join in until everyone has caught the shakes.

Guided Meditation: This activity is best with groups that are already very high-energy or active and may need a more calming physical activity.

You'll find instructions for this activity in the Planning Resources section at the end of the book.

Seeing from Other Perspectives | 20 minutes

The purpose of this activity is for participants to practice listening to another person's perspective, to strive for understanding, and to arrive at a shared vision together.

Explain and Draw

Prior to the session, the facilitator selects a relatively simple image (such as a tree, a snowman, or a shining sun). Participants will need a pen and paper. The facilitator will describe the image without saying what it is, and the participants will try to draw what they hear. Only take a couple minutes for this part of the activity, as it's basically an introduction. When ready, everyone should hold up their drawing while the facilitator shows the original image.

Next, the facilitator will select two volunteers to do the same activity in a "fish bowl" style.

Virtual Adaptation: Once the two volunteers have been selected, everyone else is invited to turn off their video so only the volunteers are visible. The facilitator will privately email or text a photo to the first volunteer and then invite them to begin describing the image for the second volunteer to draw. A timer may be used, if needed. (The rest of the group is also welcome to draw if they'd like.)

Debrief

Ask volunteers to reflect briefly on their experience. How did it feel to try to describe an image only you could see? Or to try to understand something through someone else's words? What similarities or differences do you notice in the original image and the drawing?

Invite the Whole Group to Discuss

What do we gain from sharing perspectives? (Likely themes may include communication, how people see things, expression, shared vision, or letting go of "perfection.")

Shared Vision Statement | 30 minutes

During the day's activities, group members have set intentions of being present, being honest, and showing love. They have explored who they are as individuals and have reflected on what it's like to share their unique perspectives with others. The last activity of Module One is for the group to work together to create a shared vision statement that will guide and center them as they work through the remaining modules.

To begin, the facilitator will share a blank document (**Virtual Adaptation:** or share a blank screen) and instruct the group that they will be creating a shared statement of how we can move forward in our time together. Invite participants to reflect and consider: What will it look like when we've accomplished our mission?

Invite participants to popcorn-style share words or phrases for the vision statement (**Virtual Adaptation:** by unmuting or typing in the chat). The facilitator will compile these words in the document and encourage group members to try putting together statements from these ideas. This will continue until the group arrives at a shared vision statement and the facilitator will invite a participant to read it aloud.

Wrap-up | 10 minutes

To close, the group will review the work they've done in Module One, in particular establishing shared intentions and a shared vision statement. The group is encouraged to respect the boundaries of their work together and what each person may have shared.

The facilitator will let participants know that they will all receive a follow-up email with resources and instructions, as well as any information about the next session.

Closing Prayer

Loving God,
We took the first step!
We committed to working together, to learn from one another,
and to love our neighbor throughout the process.
Guide our hearts and minds as we journey to live into your Holy,
Intentional Community. Be with each of us. Be with all of us.
In your holy name, we pray.
Amen.

Module Two: Understanding the Paths Forward

Module Two will take approximately three hours.

In this second module, the conflict begins to come into focus. Participants will name the different ways church members experience the issue's impacts—individually and collectively. They will participate in exercises and activities designed to support creative thinking, to generate possible solutions and ways forward. Significant themes should begin to emerge, and your group can discuss where the energy in the congregation is leaning.

Welcome | 10 minutes

Participants join the meeting space where calming music and video/photo imagery is playing as they gather.

Virtual Adaptation: Review basic Zoom functions and etiquette prior to beginning.

Review

When the participants have all joined, the facilitator will thank everyone for coming back to the second module and go over a brief review of what happened during the first module. The facilitator will remind the group that during the last meeting they accomplished the following:

Introduced the mission of Calm; this book offers churches the skills and tools necessary to engage in critical conversations that lead to healthy communities.

Established the boundaries to be present, be honest, and show love; the facilitator will identify ways that the group embodied these commitments.

Worked together to build an intentional community by examining who each of us is, by breaking down the virtual walls, and by working to see through differing perspectives.

Developed a shared vision of what it will look like when we are successful at creating a path forward.

The facilitator then points out: During this module, we are going to work together to understand the various paths forward. Often when groups are struggling to come together on an issue it is assumed that there are limited solutions; therefore, we are going to intentionally think through the varying potential solutions.

Describe, Interpret, Evaluate | 15 minutes

The beginning of wisdom is this: get wisdom, and whatever else you get, get insight. (Proverbs 4:7 NRSVue)

The goal of this first, whole-group exercise is to reinforce the message that it is important to see through varying perspectives in order to work together to resolve conflicts. This is an icebreaker intended to encourage conversation.

The facilitator will ask the participants to grab paper and pencil in order to take notes. Then the facilitator will show pictures, asking the group to write captions. Lastly, the facilitator will invite a few members of the group to read out their captions and will invite conversation around whether the caption described, interpreted, or evaluated the image.

It is important during this exercise to impress upon the group that it is natural to see through a personal lens or perspective, but that in order to move forward together through difficult issues we need to consider alternative perspectives.

World Cafe | 45 to 60 minutes

They were startled and terrified and thought that they were seeing a ghost.
He said to them, "Why are you frightened, and why do doubts arise in your
hearts? Look at my hands and my feet; see that it is I myself. Touch me and see,
for a ghost does not have flesh and bones as you see that I have."
(Luke 24:37-39 NRSVue)

The purpose of this activity is to identify the presenting issue and the varying ways participants relate to that issue. The focus of this activity is to listen to one another without the pressure of creating solutions. Agreement is not the goal of this activity; instead, the group will focus on capturing ideas, opinions, and underlying beliefs.

The facilitator will prepare tables with large pieces of flipchart paper and markers. Participants will sit at tables in groups of four to five. During each round, the facilitator will introduce the question the group will discuss together while capturing the information on the paper by notes or drawings. Each round will last ten to fifteen minutes. In between each round the facilitator will invite feedback for the entire group. At the beginning of each round, the participants will distribute themselves randomly among different tables.

Virtual Adaptation: The facilitator will break the group into breakout rooms on Zoom with roughly four to five people in each room. During each round, the breakout groups will discuss the questions and capture their responses on either a Google Doc, Google Forms, or Mentimeter board. Each round will last ten to fifteen minutes. In between each round the facilitator will invite feedback in the main room. At the beginning of each round, the facilitator will create new breakout rooms and assign participants randomly.

Rounds

The questions that the groups will discuss are:

1. Why are we here today?

2. Why am I here today?

3. What do both sides of this issue have in common?

The facilitator will bring the group back for debrief at the end.

Brainstorming | 40 minutes

This activity begins as a group activity but then moves into a breakout session at the end. The total time will be approximately forty minutes—twenty minutes to create the list and narrow down the options and twenty minutes for the breakout session.

The goal of this activity is to think creatively about all the possible paths forward. Groups often get stuck in the midst of conflict and think that the solutions are either X or Y. The facilitator will ask the group to think more comprehensively about all the options available to them.

This is a whole-group activity where everyone collectively works together to create a large list of possibilities. To further promote out-of-the-box thinking the facilitator may start off with an exaggerated example:

This is a process much like stream-of-consciousness intended to help us move away from thinking that there are only two options. We aren't evaluating these options yet, so don't spend much time considering whether or not the idea is good. For example, you could all give up and join the circus or you could buy a fleet of hot-air balloons and host an in-air ministry.

During the activity, the facilitator will take notes on large papers upfront and unpack suggestions as they come from participants. After several options are identified, the facilitator will invite the group to narrow down the brainstorming items into no more than four potential ways forward.

Breakout Session

The facilitator will prepare tables with large pieces of flipchart paper and markers. Participants will break into groups, one for each potential path forward. The small groups will work together to identify images that represent the option and draw them on the flipchart paper.

Virtual Adaptation: The facilitator will split the group into breakout rooms, one for each option. Once in the breakout rooms, the participants will open a Google Doc, provided by the facilitators, to add images. Images can be located via a web search and copied and pasted unto the sheet.

Break | 15 minutes

During this break, the facilitator will hang the flipchart papers up along the wall so that when the participants rejoin the space, it looks like a gallery of options.

Virtual Adaptation: The facilitator will share their screen with the documents created during the last activity.

Strengths, Weaknesses, Opportunities, Threats | 30 minutes

Think over what I say, for the Lord will give you understanding
in all things. (2 Timothy 2:7 NRSVue)

This is a reflective group activity intended for participants to evaluate the options.

The facilitator will describe a SWOT analysis: *A "SWOT analysis" is one way to evaluate options. SWOT stands for Strengths, Weaknesses, Opportunities, and Threats. In order to conduct a SWOT analysis, look closely at each one of the four options narrowed down in the brainstorming session. Consider the strengths of each option, the potential weaknesses, the opportunities that the option presents, and the threats that exist with the option.*

A tip for this activity: It can be very easy to confuse weaknesses with threats. Make the point to participants that weakness represents a negative impact; for example, "Option X might cause members to leave." However, a threat represents what might cause the option not to succeed. Example: "We don't have the resources to implement this option."

In this activity, the facilitator will lead the group through a process of attaching sticky notes to each option flipchart page. The sticky notes will each be different colors: one color each for Strengths, Weaknesses, Opportunities, or Threats.

In the first round, the facilitator passes out four pink sticky notes to each participant—one for each of the four identified options for moving forward. On each sticky note, everyone will write a strength of each of those options. Once they've finished writing, participants will stick their pink sticky notes on the corresponding option flipchart page on the wall. Once the strengths have been identified and hung up, the next round will begin. This time the group will receive green sticky notes to note the weaknesses of each option.

Next, the group will receive yellow sticky notes and the facilitator will ask the participants to consider opportunities of each option. Lastly, the group will receive orange sticky notes and will be asked to consider the threats to each option. (Note that the colors of the sticky notes don't really matter; just be sure to use a different color for each of the four SWOT categories.)

Virtual Adaptation: During each round the facilitator will display one image and then share a Mentimeter link pre-populated with four questions:

1. What is one strength of this option?

2. What is one weakness of this option?

3. What is one opportunity this option presents?

4. What is one threat to this option?

The responses will populate anonymously for the facilitator to collect and share later with the homework.

Whether meeting in person or virtually, the facilitator will ask the group to remain silent and provide a thoughtful response for each option and round. The facilitator may choose to play soft music during this activity.

Review Goal and Purpose | 10 minutes

Before concluding Module Two, the facilitator will take a moment to reflect and summarize the module's objectives:

- Understand that it is important to see complex issues from more than one perspective.
- Define the presenting issue.
- Brainstorm potential paths forward.
- Evaluate each potential path forward.

Closing Prayer

We have gathered today in your presence, Holy God, Source of Understanding and Discernment. Help us to fully embrace this journey we have undertaken. As the path we may take unfolds before us, may we embrace it with open hearts and unwavering faith. Calm our anxieties and guide us forward with your wisdom and care. Amen.

Module Three: Making Informed and Collective Decisions

Module Three will take approximately two hours for an in-person event or one and a half hours for a virtual event.

Ideally this module will take place on the same day as Module Two, with a break of one to three hours between Modules Two and Three. The purpose of this timing is because Module Three is meant to provide the opportunity for the group to take collective action, by making an informed decision around the potential paths forward brought up, discussed, and reflected upon in Module Two.

If it is the case that the group is subject to a certain decision-making process (such as a charge-conference vote) that must take place at a certain time and place, following already-established rules of order or a previously-established meeting schedule, we recommend that Module Three take place within a twenty-four-hour window before the established vote or other decision-making event. In this scenario, the purpose of Module Three would be for group members to leave the session feeling capable, confident, and prepared to make their vote. Ideally, efforts should still be made to arrange scheduling in such a way as to leave a minimal time gap between Modules Two and Three and the scheduled vote.

Leaving too much time between Modules Two and Three (or the vote) may allow for "campaigning" to happen or "camps" to form, in which individuals or small groups try to sway or influence the outcome of the decision-making process. The goal of Modules Two and Three together is to provide ample time for reflection while participants yet remain in the mind-set of occupying a sacred, community-centered space, with as minimal outside influence as possible.

Setting the Tone | 10 minutes

Welcome the group back together. Because this is the module or meeting time in which the decision-making process occurs, it is important for the facilitator to establish an environment and tone—whether physical or virtual—that remind the group they are re-entering a sacred space. This space should honor and reflect the previous work and efforts of the group: their respectful engagement, sharing, listening, and learning. Elements such as a time line, poster boards with notes, photos, or other physical tokens from previous modules may continue to be displayed, in order to call to mind these past efforts.

The facilitator will welcome the group back and walk the group through the visual time line of the modules, to remind participants where they are in the decision-making process. Participants would have spent the time between sessions thinking over the different potential ways forward, and the facilitator should acknowledge the efforts of the ongoing discernment process.

The facilitator can remind the group of their commitment to an intentional community and review the common goal. Name and identify ways that the group embodied these commitments. Explain:

Throughout our sessions together, we have worked together to build an intentional community by examining who each of us is, by breaking down our walls, then by seeing through differing perspectives. Lastly, we developed a shared vision of what it will look like when we are successful at creating a path forward.

With an eye to the future, the facilitator can also point out what comes next, after the group's decision has been made. The upcoming session—Module Four: Honoring the Process—will be an opportunity to honor the path that is being laid out toward the future through an intentional time of worship and reflection.

Identify the Collective Decision-Making Process and Transition to Action | 20 minutes

The heart of the discerning acquires knowledge, for the ears of the wise seek it out. (Proverbs 18:15 NIV)

Do not be anxious about anything, but in every situation, by prayer and petition, with thanksgiving, present your requests to God. And the peace of God, which transcends all understanding, will guard your hearts and your minds in Christ Jesus. (Philippians 4:6-7 NIV)

The goal of this module is to set the stage for informed, collective decision-making, and to ultimately decide on a path forward. All the work has been leading up to this point and the participants will likely be very anxious. The facilitator will talk about the process of collective decision-making. Explain:

The Calm *curriculum utilizes an intentional, consensus-building process to reach a decision that may or may not be any one person's best option but will hopefully be the best option available for the group. Collective decision-making through consensus ensures that every single participant has a voice in the process and that all voices are equal.*

At this point, if you have arranged so ahead of time, the pastor, clergy member, or other church leader can share a few words or short message. (This is not the time or place for surprising anyone or putting them on the spot, unprepared!)

While the clergy's message is not scripted here, ideally the message would be one of support for the process, and/or invoking a blessing on the process. By inviting the pastor or clergy member to deliver a message in Module Three, before the collective decision-making process occurs, it communicates to the congregation that church leadership is on board and the decision-making process is sanctioned and legitimate in the eyes of the church. This reassurance could be important if the group facilitator was unfamiliar to the congregation at the start of the process.

It is also critically important to the collective decision-making process that if the pastor delivers a message, they do not advocate or suggest support for a certain outcome. If circumstances suggest that a pastor or church leader is invested in a particular "side" or path forward, it may be best not to ask them to deliver a message. Alternatively, the facilitator may ask the pastor to offer the following prayer:

Creator God, God of limitless grace and compassion, be with us now as we engage in this collective decision-making process. Help us to remain present to the process knowing that we intend to make the best decision possible, not for ourselves but for the whole. We entered into this process together because we want to embody healthy and love-filled models of disagreement and problem-solving. Remind us that even though the process is hard we are developing strong and Christ-like tools for relating with one another through the good times and the hard times. Help us to be honest with our thoughts and feelings, understanding that honesty is kind. And God, help us to remember our shared goal of [INSERT GOAL HERE]. We know that in this process some will feel hurt. Please help us to see from one another's perspectives and to shoulder their hurt and care for their pain with grace, knowing that even in disagreement and pain they are an important part of our church family. Lastly, God, let this decision be the beginning of a new way forward together in love.

During this transition period, while the pastor is speaking, the facilitator can utilize this time to set up for the next activity. Which activity will follow depends on a few key factors. Different scenarios and their corresponding activities are outlined below. In the case of no message, the group may use the time to take a short break. The activity to follow should begin at the one-hour mark past the beginning of Module Three.

Once the preparations have been made and the group is set for the next activity, the facilitator can explain:

Throughout this process you have committed to be present and to be honest, and you have brainstormed many options and evaluated those options through research-based practices and through prayer and discernment. You are prepared to engage in a thoughtful and community-focused approach of collective decision-making, to find a path forward.

At this point, follow one of the three sets of following instructions for the next activity, depending on if the group is meeting in person or virtually, and whether or not the group will engage in the decision-making process as part of Module Thre, or some point in the near future.

Option One | total time: 1 hour

Scenario: Group is meeting in person, and collective decision-making CAN happen as part of Module Three.

Description of Decision-Making Tool to Be Used— Ranked Voting with Feedback | 5 minutes

Explain:

The tool we are going to use for the decision-making process is a method of ranked-choice voting. This is an anonymous feedback tool. Each participant will receive either tokens or a ballot [make this decision ahead of time]. The number of tokens received will correspond with the number of potential paths forward we identified in our previous work together. There are also that same number of voting stations set up, one for each potential path forward.

You will have the opportunity to walk around, read the statements at each voting station, and vote by indicating how you feel towards that option. Your choices will be: "I strongly agree with this path forward," "I agree with this path forward," "I am neutral towards this path forward," "I disagree with this path forward," and "I strongly disagree with this path forward."

If your group is voting with tokens, give a physical demonstration of how you'd like participants to use their tokens. For example, each voting table might be a table set up with five jars or boxes where participants can place physical objects such as marker-chips, pebbles, or marbles in the jar or box to indicate their feedback. (Note that the participants should not be able to see how many other tokens or votes have been placed in the jars or boxes as they vote.)

Votes on each path forward could alternatively be collected via a "bubble card" ballot, with the path forward written across the top, and the opportunity to pencil in one bubble to indicate their feelings of agreement, neutrality, or disagreement. Alternatively, technology-savvy groups might consider setting up a single voting station with a computer or tablet, where participants can indicate their feedback/votes for each of the paths forward on an electronic survey. (Examples and templates for these different options can be found in the Planning Resources found at the end of the book).

Depending on the level of contentiousness around the voting subject, it may be important to have a member of the facilitation team present at each voting station. Explain to participants that the facilitator will be there to provide support if there are any questions regarding the voting process itself, and to ensure only one vote is made at each station (which would be especially important if participants are voting using physical tokens). However, the facilitator should be conscientious regarding their role, as to not observe exactly how each participant is voting, but only that participants are adhering to the established voting method.

Then describe how the feedback will be tallied, to indicate the group's collective decision, once the voting has finished. For each ballot or token distribution, a vote will be tallied accordingly:

      Strong Agreement = 5 points

      Agreement = 4 points

      Neutral = 3 points

      Disagreement = 2 points

      Strong Disagreement = 1 point.

The points will be added, and the path forward receiving the highest score total will be considered the group's collective decision.

Emphasize that, upon the ending of voting, the number of votes/physical tokens cast for each path forward should equal the number of participants present. Discrepancies (too many or too few tokens) may indicate multiple votes were unfairly cast, whether intentionally or not, and a re-vote may be warranted.

Note that while using physical objects (tokens, pebbles, or marbles) to vote may make the voting process a bit more complicated regarding the setup and observation of the vote, the benefit to this method is seen in the vote-tallying process. The vote-distribution can be shared visually with the whole group once (or even as) the votes have been counted and tallied. This visual aid can be a powerful tool in representing the group's collective voice.

Finally, give participants the opportunity to ask any questions regarding the process.

Once it is clear the group is familiar and comfortable with the voting process, the group is ready to begin the Guided Prayer Walk activity. The different voting stations will be incorporated into the prayer walk journey. Incorporating the voting into a meditative prayer walk not only keeps the voting process running smoothly (since one person votes at one station at a time), but also reinforces how this important collective decision-making process is happening in a sacred space.

Guided Prayer Walk/Voting | 40 minutes

The goal of this activity is to allow participants to think about and pray about the decision-making process individually while also giving them a break from the meeting and anxiety.

Prayer stations will be set up around the room with small activities. For example, one prayer station may have a bowl of water and small pebbles. The prayer prompt may say, "Drop a pebble into the water, watch the ripples, say a silent prayer for the ripples created by this decision, both the positive results and the negative consequences." Another station may have many pictures of the community. The prayer prompt might say, "Pray for all of those outside our church doors who will benefit from this decision."

More detailed instructions for this activity can be found in the Planning Resources.

As participants journey through the prayer walk stations, this is where they will also encounter each of the voting stations. While it may be appropriate for multiple participants to visit some of the prayer stations at the same time, there should be only one person at a time at each of the voting stations. Another role of each station's observer can be to help facilitate smooth transitions from the prayer stations to the voting stations, ensuring the one-person-at-a-time voting process.

This prayer walk should ideally be set up before the session begins, and in a separate space so that the transition is easy and the group has a chance to take a break from the meeting space.

Results and Closing | 10 minutes

In the final five to ten minutes of the prayer walk (depending on the size of the group), the voting stations will close and the facilitator will tally and record the results of the voting. Once the group comes back together, the facilitator will share these results with the group. Explain:

Today you engaged in the thoughtful and community-focused approach of collective decision-making. The path forward that you chose is . . .

The facilitator will thank the group for their careful and love-filled collective decision-making and will announce the results with compassion. They will ask the group to hold their comments and reactions to respect one another, reminding the group that the upcoming module will be an opportunity to reflect on the decision, the future it points to, and the range of feelings the decision may invoke, in an intentional time of communal worship.

Before concluding Module Three, the facilitator should take a moment to reflect and summarize the unit's learning and process. Call to mind the goals and intentions participants set for themselves during Module One when creating an intentional community. Consider ending with a benediction or song.

Option Two | total time: 40 minutes

Scenario: Group is meeting virtually, and collective decision-making CAN happen as part of Module Three.

Activities for Options One and Two will be very similar, but slightly different accommodations will need to be made for virtual participation in the ranked-choice voting, as well as participation in the virtual prayer walk.

For virtual adaptation of the ranked-choice voting, a virtual survey can be created and sent out to participants, utilizing online tools such as Google Forms. The forms would be set up in such a way that participants would be able to indicate "Strong Agreement," "Agreement," "Neutrality," "Disagreement," or "Strong Disagreement" for each potential path forward. The forms can be set up so participants can remain anonymous as they vote.

To set up the virtual prayer walk, specific instructions are included in the Planning Resources. As in the in-person version of these events, voting as well as the prayer walk will happen simultaneously, to help ground the participants in the mind-set of occupying a sacred space while voting.

However, in order for this objective to be achieved, it will be important to delay the start of the voting for the first five to ten minutes, to ensure participants are able to start the prayer walk journey and enter the sacred-space mind-set before voting. Therefore, the facilitator or online-form administrator can hold off on sharing the link to the voting surveys, or allowing the survey to go live, at the immediate start of the prayer walk.

When five to ten minutes of the designated time for the prayer walk remain (provided that everyone has had the opportunity to use the surveys to vote), the facilitator will aggregate the survey data.

Note that these virtual activities are likely to take less time than their in-person counterparts; together these activities should last roughly thirty minutes.

Results and Closing | 10 minutes

When the group comes back together, the facilitator will share the ranked-choice voting results. Once the group comes back together, the facilitator will share these results with the group. Explain:

> *Today you engaged in the thoughtful and community-focused approach of collective decision-making. The path forward that you chose is . . .*

The facilitator will thank the group for their careful and love-filled collective decision-making and will announce the results with compassion. They will ask the group to hold their comments and reactions to respect one another, reminding the group that the upcoming module will be an opportunity to reflect on the decision, the future its points to, and the range of feelings the decision may invoke, in an intentional time of communal worship.

Before concluding Module Three, the facilitator should take a moment to reflect and summarize the unit's learning and process. Call to mind the goals and intentions participants set for themselves during Module One when creating an intentional community. Consider ending with a benediction or song. (In some circumstances, it might be best to join in the song before the announcement of vote.)

Option Three | total time: 30 minutes

Scenario: Group is meeting either in person or virtually, but collective decision-making CANNOT happen as part of

Module Three. (For example, a church council vote is scheduled to take place within the next twenty-four hours.)

Acknowledge the Circumstances | 5 minutes

Explain the voting process that will be taking place, as per the policy of
the church governing body, ensuring that participants clearly understand how
and when they will be able to participate.

As participants prepare to vote (ideally in the next twenty-four hours),
the facilitator will ask the group to engage in a collective time of prayer and
reflection.

Guided Prayer Walk | 20 minutes

Follow the instructions outlined above for either the in-person or virtual
prayer walk.

Closing | 5 minutes

When the group comes back together, the facilitator will thank the group
for their commitment to careful and love-filled collective decision-making.

Before concluding Module Three, facilitators will take a moment to reflect and summarize the unit's learning and process. Call to mind the goals
and intentions participants set for themselves during Module One when creating an intentional community. Consider ending with a benediction or song.

Module Four: Honoring the Process

Module Four will take approximately one hour.

Module Four is about honoring the journey that you have taken through this process and the path that is being laid out toward the future. It should be expected that for some, this is a time of celebration and excitement, while others may bring feelings of disappointment or hurt. This module is intentionally a time of worship, because through worship, the church body can humbly offer and dedicate the fruits of its labor to God, even in spite of the fruits' imperfections. Simultaneously, through worship, we invite the Holy Spirit to provide a healing presence to the church body and its many parts, as only with and through the presence of God can the church be whole.

We also want to acknowledge, in God's presence, that the outcome of the church's decision was not dictated or chosen by God. It's too easy to look back on a decision made by a human, corporate body and say, "This was God's hand in action," in an attempt to stomp out any potential opposition. The intention of this worship service is to do the opposite. Its purpose is to say we—as a human, corporate church body—came to a decision, right or wrong, good or bad. It was we who made it, and it is we who may have caused hurt or harm in the process. While we must move forward from this point, asking for God's guidance and presence along our new path, let us first pause within the presence of God as God wraps those hurt by our decision in loving arms. It may be uncomfortable to sit in the holy presence of those hurt by a decision we made, but that discomfort is important and necessary.

The theme of breath has been woven through the service. The reason for this theme is an attempt to tie a symbolic action to a physical one. Think about what happens when we breathe. Have you ever tried to calm nerves or excitement by taking a deep breath? When we breathe, we pause and create a literal space within the cavity of our chest for our lungs to expand and that life-giving exchange of oxygen into our bloodstream to occur.

This worship service is meant also to create space for reflection and to be a life-giving pause. In Module Five, we will make plans for moving forward. But first, let's create some holy space through worship.

We hope that it will be a grounding, sacred experience for your group, as they honor the work they have done together.

We have provided a worship order with adaptations for a virtual space. The service—whether virtual or in person—provides opportunities for voices of your community to be heard through spoken word, music, prayer, and writing.

To prepare for these orders of worship, the following resources and supplies are needed:

- Song books: We have made suggestions for hymns/songs from these publications: *The United Methodist Hymnal, Faith We Sing,* and *Worship & Song.* Choose the songs for worship that seem most appropriate to you, for reasons of message as well as access.

- Candle and match/lighter (or battery-operated candle).

- Altar or table for placing the candle.

- Images: nature/moving air; hands: closed and opening.

- Optional screen and projector for in-person worship.

- Word-cloud-generating website (such as mentimeter.com).

Also note the following roles:

- Leader

- Pastor/Facilitator

- Reader(s)

ORDER OF SERVICE

GATHERING

Have instrumental music and images playing, either projected on a screen or wall if possible, or as people enter the Zoom room. We suggest images of nature that depict air moving, such as wheat or trees blowing in the wind, ripples or waves in the water, and so on. While an in-person gathering does not necessarily have to take place in a formal sanctuary, do have an altar or small, centralized table for placing the lighted candle (indicated in the order of worship).

WELCOME (Facilitator)

Welcome. Today we gather for Module Four, to honor the journey we've taken together through a time of worship. Though we've come to a decision, we are not yet at our journey's end. We will meet again in holy community to make plans and create a path for moving forward. But today we will spend our time in worship, to humbly offer and dedicate the fruits of our labor—the decision we made—to God.

In offering these fruits, we are also acknowledging that we—a human, corporate church body—came to a decision. We acknowledge, in God's presence, that the outcome of the church's decision was not dictated or chosen by God. Right or wrong, good or bad, the decision was made by us, and it is we who may have caused hurt or harm in the process. And so, through worship we invite the Holy Spirit to provide a healing presence to the church body and its many parts, as only with and through the presence of God can the church be whole.

Some will enter this time with excitement and anticipation. Others may come with grief and sadness. Worship is a reminder that God welcomes us just as we are, with all that we bring. In our time together, let us honor the sacred truth that we are all children of God. Let us worship.

PROCLAMATION

Leader: Breathe in and know that God is in this space. (Light a candle and place it on the altar or table.)

Virtual Adaptation: Light a candle and set it within view of the camera, so participants can see it. Practice this beforehand, so you know where to place it.

RESPONSIVE CALL TO WORSHIP

Prepare the following call to worship using one or more readers.

Virtual Adaptation: Share a screen with the responsive call to worship written, so that others may respond. Remind readers to unmute themselves during their time to lead.

Leader: Please join us in a call to worship.

People: Breathe on me, breath of God.

Reader: We acknowledge the journey that has brought us here, a journey of struggle and of grace. Your spirit has been ever-present, just as we have strived to be present with one another. Let us feel that presence in this moment.

People: Breathe on me, breath of God.

Reader: We have sought to understand, as well as to be understood. You have given us strength to be honest with ourselves and one another. Continue to uplift us with a spirit of clarity and kindness.

People: Breathe on me, breath of God.

Reader: We give thanks for your gift of discernment and pray for your continued grace in the choices we make together in the future. We give thanks for those whom we agree and disagree with, for your grace extends to each one of us. Fill us with that grace anew.

People: Breathe on me, breath of God.

Reader: We step forward in faith and are reminded that you, the Great Shepherd, will be with each of us wherever our journey leads, as you have always been. Let us rest in the assurance of your everlasting love.

People: Breathe on me, breath of God. Amen.

OPENING SONG

The opening song should continue in the same spirit as the call to worship. If using a single refrain, we suggest singing it a few times so worshippers can feel comfortable.

Virtual Adaptation: In the virtual space, we suggest you recruit a music leader to lead any live music. Another option is to use available video recordings or have one of your church musicians create a recording for you. Our experience has been that if everyone sings unmuted at the same time, the sound becomes distorted due to limitations of the virtual space. A song leader or recording allows worshippers to sing along or simply listen.

Song suggestions:

- "Breathe" (3112)
- "The Risen Christ" (3179)
- "Honor and Praise" (2018)
- "We Have Come at Christ's Own Bidding" (2103)
- "Sanctuary" (2164)
- "Surely the Presence of the Lord" (328)
- "Breathe on Me, Breath of God" (420)
- "Holy Spirit, Come, Confirm Us" (331)
- "Spirit of the Living God" (393)

INVITATION TO GIVE TO GOD (Hand Meditation)

The following should be read slowly and deliberately, like a guided meditation, pausing after each line. The impact of this reflection is most effective when people have held their hand closed long enough to feel a sensation of release at the end. You could also share imagery of a closed, opening, and opened hand throughout, or for a **virtual adaptation**, the leader could model on their screen.

Reader: Curl your hand into a fist.

Think about all the moments of stress you've experienced during this process;

      the times you felt unheard or hurt by the statements of others;

      the things that have frustrated you;

Those things that make your stomach feel tight;

      those things that you are still worrying about.

Imagine that you hold all this in your fist.

(Pause for reflection.)

Now, slowly open your hand.

Release to God

The stresses of this process of discernment;

      the people or things who have hurt you or frustrated you.

Notice the relaxing of your hand, the unclenching of your stomach.

      Let your shoulders drop and feel the untightening of your brow.

Release the worries and the unheard or unspoken words.

Feel the sensation of release and the presence of the Holy.

"For I am the Lord your God

      who takes hold of your right hand

and says to you, 'Do not fear;

      I will help you.'" (Isaiah 41:13 NIV)

SUNG RESPONSE

This should be a song that is familiar for your worshipping community, ideally a single chorus or refrain. If less familiar, could be repeated once by the music leader.

Song suggestions:

- "Sanctuary" (2164)
- "Surely the Presence of the Lord" (328)
- "Breathe on Me, Breath of God" (420, verse 1)
- "Spirit of the Living God" (393)
- "Lord, Be Glorified" (2150)
- "Cares Chorus" (2214)

PRAYERS OF THE PEOPLE (Word Cloud)

Low tech version: Participants can simply speak their prayer request.

High tech and/or Virtual Adaptation: Before worship, choose a site with the ability to generate word clouds, such as mentimeter.com. Prepare a slide with one of the suggestions below. At this time during worship, share your online word cloud and invite worshippers to contribute their own words.

Note that this can even be done at in-person worship if a screen/projector is utilized. Participants can use their smart phones to access the word cloud site, type their response, and as a group generate a powerful, visual prayer request.

Word Cloud/Prayer Prompt:

"What are you releasing to God in prayer today?

I am releasing to God: _____."

PRAYER

Leader or Pastor: Holy God, we come before you today releasing our joys and concerns. We know you see and hear all of our prayers, even the silent ones yet on our hearts. We thank you for your presence alongside us on this journey we've been on together, and with excitement and apprehension we await the new paths that will branch out in front of us. We ask that you continue to bless us with wisdom and understanding as we move forward. Thank you for hearing our prayers today, and every day.

People: Amen.

MESSAGE

Leader or Pastor: For the message we will walk through a process called Lectio Divina, which is Latin for "Divine reading." I will read our scripture three different times and ask you to be in thoughtful reflection. Find a comfortable position, whether with your hands clasped in prayer or at your sides or with your palms up open to the Word. Take a deep breath and quiet your heart. This is your time with God. Before each reading I will offer thirty seconds of quiet reflection then ask you to focus on a specific prompt while the scripture is read.

Thirty-second pause

Leader or Pastor: Thank you, God, for the time and space to sit with your Word. Be with us during this sacred act of reflection and help us to listen for your guidance through this text.

Ezekiel 37:1-10 NRSVue

The hand of the LORD came upon me, and he brought me out by the spirit of the LORD and set me down in the middle of a valley; it was full of bones. He led me all around them; there were very many lying in the valley, and they were very dry. He said to me, "Mortal, can these bones live?" I answered, "O Lord God, you know." Then he said to me, "Prophesy to these bones and say to them: O dry bones, hear the word of the Lord. Thus says the Lord God to these bones: I will cause breath to enter you, and you shall live. I will lay sinews on you and will cause flesh to come upon you and cover you with skin and put breath in you, and you shall live, and you shall know that I am the Lord."

So I prophesied as I had been commanded, and as I prophesied, suddenly there was a noise, a rattling, and the bones came together, bone to its bone. I looked, and there were sinews on them, and flesh had come upon them, and skin had covered them, but there was no breath in them. Then he said to me, "Prophesy to the breath, prophesy, mortal, and say to the breath: Thus says the Lord God: Come from the four winds, O breath, and breathe upon these slain, that they may live." I prophesied as he commanded me, and the breath came into them, and they lived and stood on their feet, a vast multitude.

Ten-second pause

Leader or Pastor: Reflect silently on what you heard in the text.

Thirty-second pause

[Optional: Consider using this time to ask participants to say out loud what they reflected on.]

Leader or Pastor: Thank you, God, for the time and space to sit with your Word. Be with us during this sacred act of reflection and help us to consider how our work relates to this scripture.

Ezekiel 37:1-10 NRSVue

The hand of the LORD came upon me, and he brought me out by the spirit of the LORD and set me down in the middle of a valley; it was full of bones. He led me all around them; there were very many lying in the valley, and they were very dry. He said to me, "Mortal, can these bones live?" I answered, "O Lord GOD, you know." Then he said to me, "Prophesy to these bones and say to them: O dry bones, hear the word of the Lord. Thus says the Lord GOD to these bones: I will cause breath to enter you, and you shall live. I will lay sinews on you and will cause flesh to come upon you and cover you with skin and put breath in you, and you shall live, and you shall know that I am the LORD."

So I prophesied as I had been commanded, and as I prophesied, suddenly there was a noise, a rattling, and the bones came together, bone to its bone. I looked, and there were sinews on them, and flesh had come upon them, and skin had covered them, but there was no breath in them. Then he said to me, "Prophesy to the breath, prophesy, mortal, and say to the breath: Thus says the Lord GOD: Come from the four winds, O breath, and breathe upon these slain, that they may live." I prophesied as he commanded me, and the breath came into them, and they lived and stood on their feet, a vast multitude.

Ten-second pause

Leader or Pastor: Consider silently what God pointed out to you in the text regarding our conflict-resolution work together.

Thirty-second pause

[Optional: Consider using this time to ask participants to say out loud what they reflected on.]

Leader or Pastor: Thank you, God, for the time and space to sit with your Word. Be with us during this sacred act of reflection and help us to pray for our congregation's future.

Ezekiel 37:1-10 NRSVue

The hand of the LORD came upon me, and he brought me out by the spirit of the LORD and set me down in the middle of a valley; it was full of bones. He led me all around them; there were very many lying in the valley, and they were very dry. He said to me, "Mortal, can these bones live?" I answered, "O Lord GOD, you know." Then he said to me, "Prophesy to these bones and say to them: O dry bones, hear the word of the Lord. Thus says the Lord GOD to these bones: I will cause breath to enter you, and you shall live. I will lay sinews on you and will cause flesh to come upon you and cover you with skin and put breath in you, and you shall live, and you shall know that I am the LORD."

So I prophesied as I had been commanded, and as I prophesied, suddenly there was a noise, a rattling, and the bones came together, bone to its bone. I looked, and there were sinews on them, and flesh had come upon them, and skin had covered them, but there was no breath in them. Then he said to me, "Prophesy to the breath, prophesy, mortal, and say to the breath: Thus says the Lord GOD: Come from the four winds, O breath, and breathe upon these slain, that they may live." I prophesied as he commanded me, and the breath came into them, and they lived and stood on their feet, a vast multitude.

Ten-second pause

Leader or Pastor: Consider silently what prayers God lifted up in your heart.

Thirty-second pause

[Optional: Consider using this time to ask participants to say out loud what they reflected on.]

Leader or Pastor: Amen.

A COLLECTIVE RESPONSE

The opening and closing sections of this response are offered in a "pyramid" style. Each line adds a little to the line before, until the full scripture passage is read. The closing goes in reverse, with the lines becoming shorter and shorter. If possible, assign a different reader to each line (i.e. reader 1: "The Lord", reader 2: "Wait for the Lord", etc.). Another option is to alternate between two readers or between a worship leader and the congregation.

The middle section offers an opportunity for individual voices to be lifted. Prepare the reader prompts found below (those with blanks) and have them available for participants either on paper or on a screen. Provide pens or pencils for people to reflect on and complete each prompt. When joining in the response, you may decide to leave the middle section free for anyone to lift as many of their prompts as they choose. If you have a large group, we suggest each person choose one prompt to share if they feel so called.

Virtual adaptation: Invite people to complete the prompts using the chat box. The leader or pastor can then read some of the selections aloud.

Leader or Pastor: On your tables (or on the screen), you will see several prompts that are incomplete. Consider how you would finish each of these sentences. For example, someone may write, God speaks to those who are: "listening" or "ready to hear."

I invite you now, in the presence of the Holy, to reflect on and write out your responses. After a few minutes, our readers will begin with a reading of Psalm 31, after which we will share out some of our responses in a spirit of prayer.

COLLECTIVE RESPONSE (Psalm 31:24)

Reader(s):

The Lord

Wait for the Lord

All you who wait for the Lord

Take courage, all you who wait for the Lord

Let your heart take courage, all you who wait for the Lord

Be strong, and let your heart take courage, all you who wait for the Lord

Leader or Pastor: I invite you to choose and share out one of the responses you completed, as you feel so called. (Virtual: I invite you to share your responses in the chat, and we will read some of those aloud, as able.)

Reader(s): God speaks to those who are: _____.

God works through those who are: _____.

God is revealed (in/through): _____.

God gives us courage when we are: _____.

Leader or Pastor: (After people have finished sharing, the leader or pastor should verbally or non-verbally indicate to the readers to begin their closing section.)

Reader(s):

Be strong, and let your heart take courage, all you who wait for the Lord

Let your heart take courage, all you who wait for the Lord

Take courage, all you who wait for the Lord

All you who wait for the Lord

Wait for the Lord

The Lord

CLOSING SONG

Song suggestions:

- "Hymn of Promise" (707)
- "As We Go" (3183)
- "Let Our Earth Be Peaceful" (3159)
- "May You Run and Not Be Weary" (2281)
- "Sanctuary" (2164)
- "Lord, Be Glorified" (2150)
- "Grace Alone" (2162)
- "Spirit of the Living God" (393)
- "He Leadeth Me" (128)

BENEDICTION

(Extinguish the candles and read this benediction as the smoke drifts upward.)

God has called us to move forward together through a time of uncertainty. We have gathered together, laughed together, felt frustrated together, and have made a decision together. God called us as a community, and as a community we have responded. The transition of endings is sometimes hard. It is inevitable that things will end, but the Holy Spirit is still in the midst.

MUSIC AS PEOPLE EXIT

Module Five: Mapping the Path Forward

Module Five will take approximately six and a half hours.

As we begin Module Five, we have completed most of the journey. We have identified the problem, learned to see from differing perspectives, gathered a group together to take on the hard task of navigating church conflict in a healthy manner, considered our different options, and made a decision. We have honored and reflected upon the decision made and the process of reaching that decision, and we have reflected on the different effects it may have had on people in the congregation.

This process is not often an easy one. Just because a decision has been made, it does not mean that everyone involved is now completely comfortable with that decision, though ideally, everyone involved has felt comfortable within the process. Sometimes congregations reach the decision not to make a decision. The goal of this process is to not become stuck in the mire of indecision, but in rare instances the church might need to pause, allowing time and space away from the process to give it some breathing room, then returning to complete it.

In any case, the church has journeyed together and arrived at this milestone. So, what comes next?

At this point, some may think the journey—or at least their role in it—is complete. The decision has been made, and the process is finished. Yet this is not a place to stop or become stuck. We don't want to choose a path, but never move beyond the proverbial fork in the road. Once a decision has been made, without a plan, a congregation can be left feeling just as confused or uncertain as when facing the initial conflict. The goals they've set amount to little more than a wish list. We must now chart a map of the next steps so that our journey does not end with an empty decision.

This is why Module Five—mapping the path forward—is particularly useful. It's also a little different from the earlier modules.

How Module Five Is Different

This module will also take more time than the earlier modules—roughly six to seven hours. But there is a lot of movement in this module. We start together as a large group, we move out into smaller spaces, we come back as a large group, and then we move out in smaller groups again. Folks have plenty of opportunities to interact in different ways within the space. A break time is incorporated into this module so that people are able to casually mingle and chat. These opportunities to move back and forth and mingle with different people are intentional, and important. They feed energy to the work so that the Holy Spirit continues to move in what's happening. Participants are not going to be talked at for six hours. Our aim here is to provide the opportunity for engagement within the church body.

While the work can be broken up into two sessions (three- to four-hour sessions), we have found that groups tend to lose momentum and take time to get back into the flow of work when the sessions are broken up. It works best to move through the module in a single day. Because of this hefty time commitment, you may want to take a little bit of time between the end of Module Four and the beginning of Module Five. Plan just enough time and space before the fifth module so you can come back with energy and a renewed spirit to get this work done. For some groups, this may mean a week or two; for other groups, it may mean a month or two.

Module Five is also different because unlike the earlier modules, it can even be used as a stand-alone module for mapping a course of action once any kind of decision has been made, or goal has been set.

Finally, note that the participants involved in Module Five do not necessarily need to be the same team that has spent the time in the previous four modules. Hopefully many of the people involved in the earlier modules stay involved in Module Five. But think about this fifth module as an opportunity to welcome more people into this process. Individuals making up a congregation have many different gifts; there may be some for whom the conflict-centric work of the earlier modules did not feel comfortable, who instead have a gift for planning a course of action. They might be excited for the opportunity to think about new paths forward and new possibilities.

Try to draw in as many people as you can for the work of Module Five. At this point, your church has decided to undergo some sort of change, whether big or small. When any type of group is engaged in change, it's important to think about how to best manage that change. While there are many methods, techniques, and frameworks around change management, one of the most common key components is community engagement. When people are told or directed that a change has to happen, that generally doesn't work. Change is more successful with greater community buy-in.

As you can imagine: if your district, conference, or denomination instructs your church to make a change, and you feel you had no say in that decision as a congregation, it will probably be very difficult to successfully make the change. On the flip side, when you feel like you have some say in the change, and especially if you understand why the change is necessary, new processes, ideas, and practices become easier to accept.

This idea—that church members should be engaged in the decision-making process of the congregation—is at the heart of the *Calm* process.

Let us begin the work of Module Five.

Workshop Agenda

Gathering/Setup | Prior to Start

In order to provide continuity, you may decide to use the same physical location for Module Five in which Modules One through Four took place.

However, you might think about intentionally choosing a different space for the work of Module Five so that people have a different sort of mental space to go along with the different sort of task at hand.

When participants walk into the designated meeting space, there should be tables set up for large group discussion, as well as designated spaces for smaller, breakout room discussions.

Consider chair placement. A circle arrangement is best, as having participants sit in a circle indicates that this is a place where everyone is equal.

On the wall, set up a visual timeline. To create this timeline, hang multiple pieces of poster board, flipchart paper, or a long piece of butcher paper on the wall. Draw a long line across the paper, thick enough that it can be seen from all corners of the room. Where the line begins on the left, write the word 'CONFLICT,' and/or include images, drawings, or artwork to represent the conflict your church has been working to address. Then chose four points on the line, spaced roughly equidistance apart, to indicate when the four completed modules—Modules One, Two, Three, and Four—occurred. At those four points, again try to include some drawings, images, or artwork to represent the work of the four modules. Be sure that the fourth point is not placed at the end of the line; the line must continue beyond the fourth point, going out into empty space representing the future. The continuing, empty line should indicate to the participants that it's their time to pick up the mantle and their job to create what goes on that line.

Make sure participants will have access to materials such as paper, pencil, markers, sticky notes and/or tape.

Virtual Adaptation: For virtual gatherings, the timeline described above can be created and saved as an image or pdf, using whatever design software leaders are comfortable using, and shared on the presentation screen during the welcome moment and the first activity: Reflecting on the Journey. If hands on art is more your style, you might also consider drawing or creating the timeline on paper, and then taking a photo to be shared on the screen during these times.

During the Reflecting on the Journey activity, groups comfortable with tech can allow individuals to manipulate or notate the shared screen to indicate points on the timeline where they had their aha moments. If that level of comfort with tech doesn't exist for your group, individuals will still have the visual aid of the timeline in front of them, and can simply describe when and where their "aha" moments happened.

Welcome Back | 10 minutes

Start by welcoming the group into the space and reminding them why they're here, especially because now you may have new people in the group. Acknowledge the journey that has occurred and the four prior stages. Highlight their commitment as a group to being present, being kind, and being honest as well as any other important ground rules the group may have set for themselves. Finally, talk about the decision that was made and the process that led to it.

Transition to Activities

Explain: *We've been on a journey together to move out of uncertainty and in to a clearly outlined future. Let's take a few minutes to remember where we've been before we outline where we're going.*

Reflecting on the Journey | 20 minutes

The aim of this first activity is to recenter the group in the process, by having them reflect and share what has been meaningful to them about the experience so far. In this first moment that people are back in this space we are going to ask them to think about the process that has happened up until this point.

Direct individuals to take a post-it note from the tables around them and to write on it one word or phrase that has been meaningful to them throughout the process. When they finish, they are to place that post-it note on the wall, in the place they feel is most appropriate along the visual time line.

For example, for people who have been a part of the process, someone might say that an "aha" moment happened in Module One when they started to see from different perspectives. For someone else, perhaps they experienced a very poignant moment during the worship service that happened in Module Four.

For some who are present at this module but joining for the first time, this will be their first experience with this process. They will probably experience some confusion or have a lot of questions when you ask them to create their post-it note and place it along the time line on the wall. However, we still want to help ground all participants in this space. So, ask these newly joining participants to use a post-it and its placement to highlight a particular question they may have about the process. For example: "I'm most curious about this image associated with Module Three" or "I've heard folks talk about this and it sounds interesting," or "I'm confused when I hear about this."

The post-it notes can stay up throughout the day, for participants to return to any time they need to feel grounded or centered in the work set before them. The post-it notes with questions can be used to spark conversations and for sharing not only within the larger group setting when and if it may be appropriate, but also for informal, one-on-one conversations throughout the day.

Setting the Agenda | 30 minutes

The next activity in this module is important in helping the congregation understand their central role in shaping the path of the process moving forward. The large group should be sitting together in the circle arrangement. The facilitator will remind the group that they are the experts in this process and will explain there is no agenda that is created without them. Say:

> As members of your local congregation, you are the closest to what's happening within your church pews. You have the right questions. You have the right frame of reference. There is no possible way that an outside consultant, conference member, or district superintendent could come in and write an agenda for you in a way that would be more meaningful than the agenda you can write for the work that you need to do to map your course going forward.

Remind them: *This isn't the place to discuss the choice that has been made. This is the place to discuss what we have to do in order to live into this new decision. As we take the time to set our agenda, we want to remember in this moment and throughout the day to be present, to be honest, to be kind, and to welcome the ideas and voices of everyone present, whether they've been a part of the process since Module One or are joining us for the first time today.*

Once the introduction to the activity has been made, present to the group a wall-sized matrix of ten to twenty boxes, depending on the size of your group and/or the complexity of the issue at hand. (Large groups or complex issues may require fifteen to twenty boxes, and smaller groups or more straightforward issues may require ten to twelve boxes.) You could use half or full sheets of a flip chart or butcher paper, create your matrix with sheets of standard printer paper, or utilize technology in a way to project the matrix on a screen or wall. The goal is to have boxes large enough so that what is written in them can be easily seen by the larger group. If you'd like, you can label the boxes with letters (a, b, c, and so on) to help explain the process to the group, or you can leave the boxes blank for a cleaner, more streamlined look.

Then invite individuals to offer up topics for conversation around the decision that has been made. The topics will be entered into the matrix, one per box, as agenda items, written either by the individual proposing the topic or a designated scribe. The easiest way to get folks thinking about potential discussion topics is to ask them what questions they have when they think about the decision made: What are they curious about, nervous about, or excited about? As a prompt, you might offer: "I know that we've made this decision, and it's caused me to think about_____."

One example of what someone might say and write: "We've decided to start a new contemporary worship service, so now I'm thinking about the equipment that we're going to need and how we're going to afford that equipment." This could be written in the box labeled "a," thus becoming agenda item "A."

Participants should offer the questions or topics, one by one, on a volunteer basis. No one should be put on the spot, and each person should also be limited to offering a single point or question. This is important to ensure that neither the conversation nor the agenda becomes dominated by a single voice or cohort of voices.

It's normal and expected for this activity to have a slow start; people might not be ready and eager to jump up right away and participate. That's okay! Give the group the time and the space they need to get rolling, and avoid using a slow start as an opportunity for one or two people to offer multiple points or questions.

It cannot be overemphasized how important this activity is to the process, because you as the leader or facilitator have given over the authority to take up the issues that are important to the church.

Note that the goal is not to fill every single box, nor is it for every single participant to volunteer a topic. While it would be great for either, or both, of those things to happen, neither one is the endgame of the activity. What you do want to end up with is enough topics, or agenda items, to use in the next part of the process, which is considering the options. You also want to have offered everyone with questions on their mind or in their hearts the opportunity to voice and discuss one of those questions.

Virtual Adaptation: Utilize a shared screen to present a document formatted prior to the start of the session with a blank table (the number of boxes in the table will depend on the group's size; see the section above for more details). A designated scribe can type to fill in the boxes as participants either speak their ideas out loud or share them via a chat box. Alternatively, with more tech-savy groups, you might consider sharing a link to the document via Google Docs or the like, so participants can enter their ideas directly into the shared document.

If you do use a shared document, make sure you save an original version of the document(s) after each activity and create copies to share with small groups in breakout rooms in the subsequent activities. Continue to use shared documents and breakout rooms whenever small group activities are indicated.

Considering the Options | 140 minutes

For this activity, the large group will break into smaller groups: one group dedicated to each of the agenda items generated in the previous activity. This means that you will also need to have prepared potential workspaces for these small groups. Small group workspace might be at tables, church classrooms or study rooms, or even outside if it's appropriate. While the space itself depends on your context, it is important to have places prepared and preferably noted in writing as participants break into the small groups (that is, "agenda item a, table 1"). Make sure all participants understand when and where each group is to be working; that way anyone who wants to move to a new topic during the course of the activity knows where to go to do so. It may be useful to have volunteers stationed throughout this activity to help point participants to different workspaces.

Participants are asked to self-select the group they would like to participate in, depending on their interest in and energy for the group's determined topic. Participants can stay in the same group for the entire activity time period or split their time between different groups and topics as they would like.

Tell the group: *You don't need to stay in any one space for the entire time. You can move freely in this exercise as the spirit leads and put yourself in the place where you feel like your ideas, knowledge, and expertise could be the most helpful or where you have the most passion for the conversation.*

Note that while the most straightforward course of action might be to run each group for the full time allotted, it is not necessary. This could be an especially important point to note for congregations with limited working space.

As an example, let's say there are a hundred people who attend this event, and the group generated ten agenda items in the previous activity. Additionally, you decided that you will use the full 140 minutes. That means you must designate ten small-group spaces and ask those one hundred individuals to split up into those spaces as they like. Maybe you have ten spaces to use, so all the topics are discussed at once, with all participants milling around, joining and leaving the discussions at random. Or maybe instead you open five spaces at a time, discuss five of the agenda items (one item in each of the five spaces) for seventy minutes, then discuss the remaining five items in the second seventy-minute stretch. Or maybe you only have two large spaces, and discuss five of the items in each room, for about twenty-five minutes each. You can decide what arrangement fits your context best, based on the number of participants, number of topics, available space, and interest or participation level of the participants.

The goal of this activity is to provide the groups enough time and space to dive into deep and productive conversations around topics inspired by the group's questions, worries, and excitements.

The groups should be provided ample time to consider questions such as:

- What are the most important ideas that we have around this topic?
- What are the most salient discussion points that we don't want lost?
- What are some of the recommendations that we have for this question?
- What are the next steps?
- Who could be the responsible party to make sure these steps are taken?
- What do we need to do to address any concerns?

As a facilitator or team of facilitators, you may decide to provide this, or a similar, list of questions to the groups in order to encourage a robust discussion. However, you may also decide not to provide the groups with any discussion prompt, and let the conversations evolve naturally. To make this decision, consider the people's willingness to engage in discussion thus far in the process. For this activity, less facilitation is preferable. But if a hands-off approach means your groups will feel uncomfortable or confused, give them the support needed to have productive, lively conversations. As an individual facilitator or a facilitation team, have a strategy around how you will divide your time and attention amongst the different group discussions, to keep track of the progress being made in the different discussion spaces and to offer light support when necessary.

Another integral part of this activity is ensuring that in each group discussion there is a rapporteur—that is, someone to make notes or create illustrations, charts, pictures, or any other type of visible representation of the group's work that can be shared with the larger group during the debriefing activity to follow. You will also ask the small groups to post their notes, illustrations, and charts on the wall by the visual time line from the very first activity, so that people get a chance to check out the notes of discussions that happened in rooms they couldn't be in. Ask the groups to self-select this person or people, and make sure there are writing/drawing materials readily available at all the small-group work spaces. Assigning rapporteurs ahead of time should not be necessary.

Example Scenario:

Let's continue using the example of the decision to start a new, contemporary worship service, with the agenda item of sourcing the appropriate technology. Imagine the discussion in the small-group discussion generated these notes:

- Work with local conference resources.
- Utilize a local high school that has a recording studio.
- Look for equipment that could be bought cheaply from Google Marketplace or Facebook Marketplace.
- Other churches in the area with technical savvy can tell us about the appropriate equipment needed.

Recommendations:

- Use a grant from the conference to buy tech for our church.

Responsible parties:

- Who can find and fill out a grant application?

The goal of this activity is not to end with a comprehensive plan forward just yet. It's more of a brainstorming session, to get ideas and questions down on paper. Your goal should be to end the activity with lots of ideas and possibilities, and a large group warmed up and ready to discuss in even further detail.

But first, let's give them a break!

Break | 60 minutes

After all of that exciting, invigorating idea generation, people will need a break. An hour break with a light meal is ideal. However, if you've decided to break this work into two days, this would also be a great place to end work for day one.

During the break, encourage participants to enjoy their food, have some exercise, and talk about something that does not pertain to the work at hand. You will probably have groups that continue to talk about what happened in their discussion space. So just ask that if they are going to continue any of the group-work discussions, to make notes and add the notes to the wall so their further ideas are captured as well. This is also true if day one of work stops at this point. Encourage participants to take note of any ideas or discussions that happen outside the work space, and add the notes to the wall at the start of day two.

Debrief | 20 minutes

When you reconvene after the break or at the start of the second day, gather once again as a large group in a circular formation.

The first activity for the reconvened large group is a debriefing session.

First, welcome the group back again. Ask for representatives from each of the small-group breakout rooms to provide a brief overview of what happened in their discussion and to read their notes out loud so that the whole group can hear the ideas generated by the small group.

As the facilitator, consider the number of groups that must report, and keep an eye on the time. Of course, you can add some time for this activity in the case of a very large group. Nevertheless, you want to keep this activity moving along, without much back-and-forth discussion. This activity should simply be a reading and a recount of the notes that are already available on the walls.

Ideally, people have had a chance to read through the wall notes, but we still want the notes and ideas to be said out loud so that people can digest the information in a different way. This process of recapping and debriefing reinforces the different ways that people digest the information: visually, orally, and with repetition.

Identify Themes | 20 minutes

The next activity is also for the large group and should also happen fairly quickly. The goal of this activity is to start identifying patterns and themes from among the notes and presentations of the small-group discussions. You can even combine some of the work of this activity with the previous activity, by asking the representatives of the small groups to try and name some themes that came out of the group discussions.

This activity tends to get easier as it progresses because the first groups to present have less to work with, in order to identify patterns. So, if the first groups struggle a little to identify larger themes, that is okay! As more groups present, patterns should begin to emerge.

As these patterns emerge and themes are identified, task the large group to consider these different themes and think about ways to group patterns and themes until only three or no more than four larger, overarching themes are identified and agreed upon by the large group.

Example Scenario:

In the contemporary worship service example, potential conversations may have been:

- Who is going to run the sound board at this contemporary worship service?
- Who might be the worship leader?
- Who would be responsible for recruitment for this event?
- Who can provide childcare?

At first glance these conversations may seem very different, but they could potentially be grouped under the overarching theme of staffing/personnel.

After forty minutes spent in a large group, that is roughly 20 minutes debriefing and 20 minutes identifying themes, it is time to split back into small groups, in order to create specific goals.

Goal Creation | 40 minutes

Throughout Module Five, our work plan has taken the shape of a funnel, as we have been moving from big, broad ideas, then grouping them into narrower themes. Now we need to generate specific goals and action steps.

At this point, the group should have reached a consensus, through their discussion, on ideally three but absolutely no more than four overarching themes, which we will now call the "priority areas."

For the example scenario we've been using, perhaps those themes/priority areas identified are staffing, technology, and liturgy.

Once again, ask the larger group to self-select into smaller groups, one group for each of the priority areas identified.

In order to create goals and action steps, the groups can draw upon all the resources generated throughout the process: the notes and drawings from the previous activities and the themes. Each of the groups should have access to these resources at their workspaces.

Over the course of the next forty minutes, the groups will identify three to four S.M.A.R.T goals for each priority area. S.M.A.R.T goals are goals that are specific, measurable, achievable, relevant, and time-bound.

For example, a goal for the example scenario of getting technology for our new worship service, is not S.M.A.R.T. While it is perhaps achievable and relevant, it is not specific, measurable, or time-bound. However, this goal is S.M.A.R.T.: "We will get a sound board (specific) within the next thirty days (time-bound) for our worship service." It's still achievable and relevant. By including the thirty-day time frame, it's also a measurable goal; at the end of thirty days, you will be able to measure if you were successful (there's a soundboard at the church) or not (there is no soundboard).

A note for facilitation: If there seems to be some confusion within any of the groups around S.M.A.R.T. goals, a facilitation strategy might be to encourage the groups to think of their goals in any form—S.M.A.R.T. or otherwise. Then when the groups share and debrief their work with the larger group, the large-group-mind can help turn broader goals into S.M.A.R.T. goals.

The groups will not only come up with three to four specific goals but also come up with four to five action steps necessary in order to achieve each of the goals. Groups may find that many of these action steps can be drawn from the earlier group discussions around the original agenda items, as the priority areas and goals should still be related to those initial discussions. Therefore the forty-minute time frame for this activity is appropriate; however, facilitators should monitor the progress of the groups, and more time can be added for the activity if necessary. Add more time judiciously, though. If there's a group with only one or two goals while the other groups have finished, you may still want to call time. While three or four goals is the aim of this activity, consider it a guideline rather than a steadfast rule.

An important point to make to the groups about their work: it may be that final authority regarding certain aspects of proposed plans will rest with church staff, board leadership, or conference leaders. Decisions affecting church budgets and staffing are a prime example of this; a workshop group likely can't make any decisions that would affect the church budget or staffing because there may not be room for budget lines to be adjusted drastically until the next fiscal year.

However, the groups can create or suggest guiding principles for work to be done by the leaders or committee members in their official capacity. In other words, decisions made or paths forward selected by the groups today are in no way binding to the church. But the day's outputs are of significant importance, as they will provide a clear and crucial perspective to those who can make binding decisions as to what the church body hopes to see happen. Having the pastor or someone on the leadership team present to make this point—that the leaders are welcome to, and anxious to have, this perspective of the church body—can go a long way in assuring the group that their work and input is meaningful in shaping the church's path forward, and in helping the church live into the decision made in the earlier module.

Presenting the Path | 20 minutes

Once the groups are ready, bring everyone back to the large-group setting. Now each of the small groups will be given the opportunity to present their work to the larger group—the steps they've identified as part of the path forward.

Additionally, the full group will have a chance to give some feedback on the goals and action steps. The goals may be tweaked or amended based on the feedback and general consensus.

Creating the Map | 30 minutes

You may decide to skip this activity, based on time constraints, and move from presenting the path straight to the closing. However, a full-circle moment that works especially well if you have lots of visual processors in the group is to return to the time line from the beginning of the day. Bring the group's attention to the time line once again and make the point:

> Our group started the day [or yesterday] here, reflecting on the path we've journeyed along to make our decision. [Point out the long line going out into empty space, representing the future.] When we started, the future was a mystery. Now we have a better idea of what it may look like; now we have a map for our path forward.

At this point, depending on the time as well as your group's sensibilities, you can take some of the notes, illustrations, themes, and/or goals and post them along the blank space on the time line, indicating the future.

Alternatively, you can give the group thirty minutes to work on creating some kind of artwork or visual representation to place on the time line when they've finished, indicating a map or path forward. Let the group divide themselves in whatever way they see fit—small groups, pairs, a large group, or any way that allows the best chance to reflect and create. Just make sure there is an ample supply of materials (paper, markers, pencils, scissors, glue, etc.) easily accessible to all.

You can therefore end the day with a great visual representation of the path to move forward. If possible, leave the completed time line or at least this final "creating the map" artwork on display in the church for a couple of weeks, to share with the larger congregation about the Calm workshop and outcomes.

Closing | 10 minutes

The very last thing to do is to have a closing ceremony. With the large group back together one final time, thank them for their time, effort, and dedication to the process. Remind the group:

At the end of the day, here is what we have accomplished: We created agenda items based on what this group found to be important. We created time and space for people to ideate and be in community with one another. We identified the major themes repeatedly showing up around the work that needs to be done. And we created goals so that we may achieve success with this new path indicated by our map forward.

Hopefully the group is excited about the outcomes they've produced. Depending on the goals and action steps created, you may need to delicately remind them of the point made earlier in the day: that decisions made or paths forward selected by the groups today are in no way binding to the church. But the day's outputs are of significant importance, as they will provide a clear and crucial perspective to those who can make binding decisions as to what the church body hopes to see happen.

Finally, ask the group to respond to this prompt out loud, one by one:

"When we first came here, I felt _____. And now I feel _____."

If you have too large of a group, you can alternatively have people turn to their neighbors and answer the prompt together in pairs or groups of three.

The goal is to be able to see the trajectory of the process the group has journeyed on throughout the day.

Finally, end the day in prayer.

Closing Prayer

Lord, we offer our heartfelt gratitude for your presence with us today.
You were present in our conversations,
In our hearts as we dreamed,
In our hands as we planned.
Bless our work today as we begin to live into our new path.
Let us journey together—no matter the terrain—
knowing that you are our guide and that we are your Holy Community.
Amen

———————

This process may have begun with conflict, but at its end, with this fifth module, your church has not only made a decision on how to move forward but also produced a concrete action plan and identified the steps necessary for enacting that plan.

This process should revitalize church members and instill in them the confidence that they can be a healthy congregation now and into the future, with healthy behaviors and the tools they need to address church conflict. All of this together fosters hope and momentum moving forward.

Planning Resources

As you prepare to use this curriculum in your church, you will want quick access to additional resources, templates, and more detailed descriptions for some of the activities found in the modules. In this chapter, you will find some of these additional resources. Other resources are available on the *Calm* landing page:

www.cokesbury.com/calm-book

Online Resources

Mentimeter: Utilizing mentimeter.com allows you to design live survey polls, word clouds, and audience participation prompts. This website is useful for leading several of the activities in the virtual adaption of this curriculum, but it can be used for in-person meetings as well.

The Session Lab: This is a useful website (sessionlab.com) that provides descriptions and instructions for hundreds of group activities should you need additional ideas or resources for planning workshops with your congregation.

Guided Meditation

Invite everyone in the group to find a quiet and comfortable space in which to sit or lie down, as they prefer. If possible, dim the lights and ensure the room is free from distractions (cell phones, screens, outside noise, etc). Emphasize that there is no right or wrong way to experience meditation. Start the meditation by helping participants connect with their bodies and the present moment: asking them to focus on their breath, to feel the weight of their bodies on the ground or chair, and become aware of any sensations or sounds around them. Encourage participants to set an intention for the meditation session—a word or phrase that represents what they want to cultivate or let go of during the practice. This could be "peace," "clarity," or "let go of stress." Using a calm and soothing voice, guide participants to relax their bodies, breathe deeply, and let go of any tension or thoughts that arise. You may want to incorporate imagery, such as a peaceful natural setting or a warm, healing light, to enhance the experience. Then have the group experience a few minutes of silence, giving participants space to explore their own inner experiences. After 3-5 minutes of silence, gradually bring the meditation to a close by gently guiding participants back to the present moment. Invite them to slowly bring awareness back to their bodies, wiggle their fingers and toes, and open their eyes when they feel ready. If time permits provide an opportunity for participants to share their experience or any insights gained.

Guided Prayer Walk Instructions

For this activity, you will need to set up stations in a variety of places around your church. You will also need to create a map so that participants know where they can go to find the next prayer activity. It is nice to have quiet music playing and to remind participants that this is meant to be a quiet time for themselves and God. If any of the activities do not work in your physical location, it is okay to leave them out. Each station includes a scripture or prayer for meditation.

Supplies needed will be:

- A prayer activity card for each station

- Rocks

- Slips of paper

- Bowls

- Pencils

- A stapler

- A few stations require a specific song to be played

- Wildflower packets

- Sand

- A lit fire in a fireplace

A sample map of stations is available online at the Abingdon Press *Calm* landing page. *(Note that the numbers are included to easily differentiate the different stations; they are not meant to suggest an order for visiting the different stations.)*

Station 1: Child of God

This station should have Mark Miller's song "Child of God" playing on repeat.

Spend some time in prayer thanking God for all the ways you identify and all of your unique gifts and skills. Write a word that describes yourself.

For in Christ Jesus you are all children of God through faith. (Galatians 3:26 NRSVue)

I am a_____.

I am a child of God.

Station 2: Sanctuary

Close your eyes and envision yourself sitting in the church sanctuary. Think of all the church members who sat in those pews before you. Say a prayer for the members who will sit in these pews in the future.

> God said, "This is the sign of the covenant that I make between me and you and every living creature that is with you, for all future generations: I have set my bow in the clouds, and it shall be a sign of the covenant between me and the earth." (Genesis 9:12-13 NRSVue)

Station 3: Prayer for Worries

This station requires paper and a pencil.

Life can be scary at times. There are big things happening in the world and it is okay to bring all your feelings to God, big or small. Write a worry on a slip of paper. Crumple it up and keep it just for yourself and God. Then throw it into the garbage and give that worry to God. Lastly, read this prayer silently to yourself:

> God, when everything around me seems to be on the brink of collapse, guide me to solid ground. When I believe I cannot go any further, help me to persevere. Guide me tenderly toward the path I should follow; lead me to find tranquility and safety. Despite the chaos prevailing in the world, draw me nearer to your presence. Amen.

Station 4: Holy Ground

> For where two or three are gathered together in my name, there am I in the midst of them. (Matthew 18:19 KJV) (Even virtually!)

Take off your shoes. You are standing on holy ground. Rub your soles along the ground and feel the earth beneath your feet.

Pray this silent prayer:

> Holy Creator, mesmerize us with the wonders of your creation.
>
> Grace us as we walk on your sacred soil.
>
> Stir and incite us. Help us to consider our part in your design.
>
> Astonish us with your radiant splendor.
>
> Amen.

Station 5: Healing Prayer

Pick up something rough near you and hold it in your hand. Feel its weight, its rough exterior, its sharp edges. As you hold your object, pray for the healing of the world.

> He gives strength to the weary and increases the power of the weak. (Isaiah 40:29 NIV)

Station 6: Prayer for Action

This station should have the song "Sanctuary" playing.

Respond to the link and write one way you plan to work for goodness in the world. Add your commitments to the commitments of others, then pray for the Lord to prepare you to be a sanctuary.

> He has told you, O mortal, what is good,
>   and what does the LORD require of you
> but to do justice, and to love kindness,
>   and to walk humbly with your God? (Micah 6:8 NIV)

Station 7: Prayer for Neighbors

If you can, open your window. Take a deep breath. Close your eyes and listen to the wind in the trees. Smell the fresh air and listen to the sounds of your community. Know that you are standing with God. Say a silent prayer for your neighborhood.

> The wind blows where it chooses, and you hear the sound of it,
> but you do not know where it comes from or where it goes. So
> it is with everyone who is born of the Spirit. (John 3:8 NRSVue)

Station 8: Prayer for Church Staff

This station should have wildflower seed packets. The station should be outside in a place where it would be okay for wildflowers to grow.

The church staff works tirelessly to provide a faithful, loving, environment for all church members. Plant a flower in honor of their hard work and as a way of saying thank you. Then say a prayer for them.

> And let us not grow weary of doing good, for in due season we will reap, if we do not give up. (Galatians 6:9 ESV)

Station 9: Ripples

This station should have a pile of small stones and a large bowl of water.

Pick up a pebble and then drop it gently into the bowl of water. Observe the outward ripples, and then read this prayer:

> Lord, please help us to notice how our actions impact others. Remind us to be mindful and courteous in all that we do, striving to always walk in your footsteps and treat others with love.

Station 10: Prayer of Resiliency

This station should have a pile of flat stones. Before the prayer walk, you should stack a couple as an example.

Pick up a stone and add it to the ebeneezer. Ebeneezers were used in the Bible to remember victories. Say a prayer celebrating the fact that you've been resilient through tough times.

> Then Samuel took a stone and set it up between Mizpah and Shen. He named it Ebenezer, saying, "Thus far the LORD has helped us." (1 Samuel 7:12 NIV)

Station 11: Prayer of Thanks

This station should have a bowl of sand.

Pick up some sand from the bowl and rub it between your fingers. Think of the millions of ways God is at work in our lives. Next, pray, "God thank you for the ways you are at work in . . ."

> The steadfast love of the LORD never ceases;
>   his mercies never come to an end.
> (Lamentations 3:22 ESV)

Virtual Prayer Walk Adaptation

The main difference from the in-person version and the virtual adaptation is that instead of participants wandering through the prayer walk space and choosing a station at their discretion, you will lead virtual participants through the activity one prayer at a time. It is important to note that this version requires participants to collect supplies and have them ready beforehand. It is important to let participants know about the items they will need to gather in their preparation for the module. You may even consider putting together care packages with the items needed and providing them for participants.

This may a good activity to recruit help from the pastor to read out the prompts for each prayer. In that way, the facilitator can introduce the activity, flip through slides, and act as a guide.

Supplies you will need for this activity:

- Timer

- Slide deck with all the prayer prompts and scriptures written on separate slides

- YouTube link of Mark Miller's song "Child of God"

- Picture of your church's sanctuary

- Paper

- Pencils

- Stone or small, rough object

- YouTube link to the song "Sanctuary"

- Mentimeter link with the prompt "What is one way you plan to work for goodness in the world?"

- Thank-you cards

- Pebbles

- Flat stones

- Picture of an ebeneezer

- Sand

Facilitator: This next activity is a time for careful reflection. It is an individual activity so feel free to mute yourself and turn off your camera. There will be eleven separate prayer prompts where we will ask you to pray in various ways and reflect on various topics. Now is the time to gather the prayer journey supplies that you gathered [or were provided for you]. Have them ready as we move through the prayers together. We will pray together for two minutes on each prompt to give you enough time to quiet your heart and mind. Let's begin with a minute of silent reflection.

During the silent reflection the facilitator and host will prepare the first prompt. The facilitator or pastor should set a timer for two minutes after each prompt is read. This is to make sure that each prayer offers enough time for the participants to be in conversation with God. Though, it is important to make sure that the timer is only for the facilitator and that it is silent.

Prayer 1: Child of God

Time: two minutes

This station should have Mark Miller's song "Child of God" playing on repeat.

Pastor or Facilitator: Spend some time in prayer thanking God for all the ways you identify and all of your unique gifts and skills. Write, "I am a _____," then list all the ways you identify. Lastly, write, "I am a child of God." Reflect of the fact that, no matter how you describe yourself, you are loved by God.

> For in Christ Jesus you are all children of God through faith. (Galatians 3:26 NRSVue)
>
> I am a _____.
>
> I am a child of God.

Prayer 2: Holy Ground

Time: two minutes

Display a picture of your church's sanctuary on the slide deck.

Facilitator or Pastor: *Close your eyes and envision yourself sitting in the church sanctuary. Think of all the church members who sat in those pews before you. Say a prayer for the members who will sit in these pews in the future.*

> God said, "This is the sign of the covenant that I make between me and you and every living creature that is with you, for all future generations: I have set my bow in the clouds, and it shall be a sign of the covenant between me and the earth." (Genesis 9:12-13 NRSVue)

Prayer 3: Prayer for Worries

Time: two minutes

This station requires paper and a pencil.

Facilitator or Pastor: *Life can be scary at times. There are big things happening in the world and it is okay to bring all your feelings to God, whether big or small. Write a worry on a slip of paper. Crumple it up and keep it just for yourself and God. Then throw it into the garbage and give that worry to God. Lastly, read this prayer silently to yourself:*

> God,
> Help me to stand when I feel I'm about to fall;
> help me to carry on when I feel I can't take another step.
> Lead me gently in the direction that I should go;
> lead me into a place of peace and security.
> Even while the world around me is full of turmoil,
> bring me closer to you.
> Amen.

Prayer 4: Holy Ground

Time: two minutes

Participants will either need to take off their shoes or rub their feet on the floor with their shoes on.

> For where two or three are gathered together in my name, there am I in the midst of them. (Matthew 18:19 KJV) (Even virtually!)

Facilitator or Pastor: *Take off your shoes or focus on your feet. You are standing on holy ground. Rub your soles along the ground and feel the earth beneath you then pray the prayer on the slide silently to yourself.*

> God of fire and burning bush, Come meet us on holy ground. Come sit with us. Inspire and challenge us. Dazzle us with your creation. God of surprises, come meet us on holy ground. Come sit with us. Move and provoke us. Startle us with your beauty. Amen.

Prayer 5: Healing Prayer

Time: two minutes

Participants will need a small, rough object to hold, like a stone.

Facilitator or Pastor: *Pick up something rough near you and hold it in your hand. Feel its weight, its rough exterior, its sharp edges. As you hold your object, pray for the healing of the world.*

> He gives strength to the weary and increases the power of the weak. (Isaiah 40:29 NIV)

Prayer 6: Prayer for Action

Time: two minutes

This station should have the song "Sanctuary" playing.

Facilitator or Pastor: *Respond to the Mentimeter link [or type in the chat] one way you plan to work for goodness in the world. Add your commitments to the commitments of others, then pray for the Lord to prepare you to be a sanctuary.*

> He has told you, O mortal, what is good,
>
>> and what does the LORD require of you
>
> but to do justice and to love kindness
>
>> and to walk humbly with your God? (Micah 6:8 NIV)

Prayer 7: Prayer for Neighbors

Time: two minutes

Pastor or Facilitator: *If you can, open your window. Take a deep breath. Close your eyes and listen to the wind in the trees. Smell the fresh air and listen to the sounds of your community. Know that you are standing with God. Say a silent prayer for your neighborhood.*

> The wind blows where it chooses, and you hear the sound of it, but you do not know where it comes from or where it goes. So it is with everyone who is born of the Spirit. (John 3:8 NRSVue)

Prayer 8: Prayer for Church Staff

Time: two minutes

This prayer requires thank-you cards.

Facilitator or Pastor: The church staff works tirelessly to provide a faithful, loving, environment for all church members. Write a note of appreciation for their hard work. Then say a prayer for them.

> And let us not grow weary of doing good, for in due season we will reap, if we do not give up. (Galatians 6:9 ESV)

Prayer 9: Ripples

Time: two minutes

This prompt requires a pebble and a glass of water.

Facilitator or Pastor: Pick up a pebble and then drop it gently into your cup of water. Observe the outward ripples, and then read this prayer:

> Lord, please help us to notice how our actions impact others. Remind us to be mindful and courteous in all that we do, striving to always walk in your footsteps and treat others with love.

Prayer 10: Prayer of Resiliency

Time: two minutes

This prayer should have a slide with a picture of an ebeneezer—stones stacked in commemoration of divine assistance. Participants should also have two to three flat stones that they can stack while praying.

Facilitator or Pastor: *Pick up a stone and add it to the ebeneezer. Ebeneezers were used in the bible to remember victories. Say a prayer celebrating the fact that you've been resilient through tough times.*

> Then Samuel took a stone and set it up between Mizpah and Shen. He named it Ebenezer, saying, "Thus far the Lord has helped us." (1 Samuel 7:12 NIV)

Prayer 11: Prayer of Thanks

Time: two minutes

This station should have a bowl of sand.

Facilitator or Pastor: *Pick up some sand from the bowl and rub it between your fingers. Think of the millions of ways God is at work in our lives. Next, pray, "God thank you for the ways you are at work in . . ."*

> The steadfast love of the Lord never ceases;
>   his mercies never come to an end.
> (Lamentations 3:22 ESV)

References

Several facilitation techniques listed in the book were modeled after activities originally developed by other authors, researchers, clergy members, and more. This page captures those references.

Describe, Interpret, Evaluate (Used in Module Two): Originally developed by Bennett, J. M., Bennett, M. J., & Stillings, K. (1977).

World Cafe (Used in Module Two): Originally developed by Juanita Brown and David Isaacs, in the early 1990s.

SWOT Framework (Used in Module Two): The SWOT framework was first described in detail in the late 1960s by Edmund P. Learned, C. Roland Christiansen, Kenneth Andrews, and William D. Guth.

Setting the Agenda & Considering the Options (Used in Module Five): Inspired by *Open Space Technology: A User's Guide Book* by Harrison Owen.

Acknowledgments

This material would not have been possible without the motivation and support of others. Specifically, we would like to thank Carl Gladstone for believing in us and encouraging our team to create the curriculum, and Sonya Luna for her gift of time and consultation as we developed the curriculum.

CPSIA information can be obtained
at www.ICGtesting.com
Printed in the USA
LVHW050140240623
750323LV00004B/16

9 781791 030247